JUST GO
FOR IT!

DAME KELLY HOLMES

with Linda Bird

JUST GO FOR IT!

6 Simple Steps to Achieve Success

HAY HOUSE

HAY HOUSE

Australia • Canada • Hong Kong • India
South Africa • United Kingdom • United States

First published and distributed in the United Kingdom by:
Hay House UK Ltd, 292B Kensal Rd, London W10 5BE.
Tel.: (44) 20 8962 1230; Fax: (44) 20 8962 1239. www.hayhouse.co.uk

Published and distributed in the United States of America by:
Hay House, Inc., PO Box 5100, Carlsbad, CA 92018-5100. Tel.: (1) 760 431
7695 or (800) 654 5126; Fax: (1) 760 431 6948 or (800) 650 5115.
www.hayhouse.com

Published and distributed in Australia by:
Hay House Australia Ltd, 18/36 Ralph St, Alexandria NSW 2015.
Tel.: (61) 2 9669 4299; Fax: (61) 2 9669 4144. www.hayhouse.com.au

Published and distributed in the Republic of South Africa by:
Hay House SA (Pty), Ltd, PO Box 990, Witkoppen 2068.
Tel./Fax: (27) 11 467 8904. www.hayhouse.co.za

Published and distributed in India by:
Hay House Publishers India, Muskaan Complex, Plot No.3, B-2,
Vasant Kunj, New Delhi – 110 070. Tel.: (91) 11 4176 1620;
Fax: (91) 11 4176 1630. www.hayhouse.co.in

Distributed in Canada by:
Raincoast, 9050 Shaughnessy St, Vancouver, BC V6P 6E5.
Tel.: (1) 604 323 7100; Fax: (1) 604 323 2600

© Kelly Holmes, 2011

The moral rights of the author have been asserted.
All rights reserved. No part of this book may be reproduced by any
mechanical, photographic or electronic process, or in the form of a
phonographic recording; nor may it be stored in a retrieval system,
transmitted or otherwise be copied for public or private use, other than for
'fair use' as brief quotations embodied in articles and reviews, without prior
written permission of the publisher.

The author of this book does not dispense medical advice or prescribe the
use of any technique as a form of treatment for physical or medical problems
without the advice of a physician, either directly or indirectly. The intent of
the author is only to offer information of a general nature to help you in your
quest for emotional and spiritual well-being. In the event you use any of the
information in this book for yourself, which is your constitutional right, the
author and the publisher assume no responsibility for your actions.

A catalogue record for this book is available from the British Library.

ISBN 978-1-84850-255-0

Printed and bound in the UK by CPI Mackays, Chatham ME5 8TD

All of the papers used in this product are recyclable, and made from wood
grown in managed, sustainable forests and manufactured at mills certified to
ISO 14001 and/or EMAS

CONTENTS

Introduction   vii

Chapter 1 – Setting Goals (Ones You're   **1**
                Really Going to Reach)

Chapter 2 – Getting Organised: Fast-track   **31**
                Success with the Right Preparation

Chapter 3 – Thinking Positive: Secrets to   **61**
                Staying Confident

Chapter 4 – Overcoming Obstacles: **97**
                The Will to Win

Chapter 5 – Motivation Secrets: How to Tap   **145**
                into Your Willpower

Chapter 6 – Enjoying the Journey: **171**
                The Rewards of Perseverance

Conclusion   **201**

INTRODUCTION

I don't know about you, but without a goal or direction, I don't feel I'm living my life.

I'm one of those people who sets high goals for herself and is always searching for a new challenge, or a different direction.

There are people out there who are unaware of who they are or what they want out of life, or who may just have lost the will to do anything. There are also plenty of people I've met who, like me, are motivated, always looking for a new venture and not afraid to give their all to achieve it. The hard part for us all can be working out *what* it is or *how* to do it...

I've been lucky. I am driven and focused and my commitment to my goals has certainly paid off. From the age of 14 I dreamed about being an Olympic champion. I spent years single-mindedly trying to reach that dream – 20 years in fact of learning about myself and challenging myself, undergoing hard training sessions and pushing my body to exhaustion.

During that time I experienced heartbreaking setbacks and disappointments alongside amazing victories and achievements, both in my working life in the Army and in my sporting career. For many of those years I was thinking of little else but being the best.

Yes, it paid off. Winning two Olympic gold medals is an incredible achievement; it's something most sportspeople dream about (including me). Those medals are more than I could ever have asked for, the richest reward of all. I'll never be able to describe the feeling of euphoria as I stood on that rostrum to receive my medals.

Being an Olympic champion has changed my life and opened many doors to me. It has enabled me to meet many inspiring people, and enjoy extraordinary experiences. And yes, it has provided me with certain financial rewards (though, believe me, not as many as people might assume). I'm certainly not paid enough to sit in the garden and twiddle my thumbs all day! (Although I probably wouldn't anyway.)

The truth is, after many years of training and competing, my life has been taking a different direction. Athletics was a route to life-changing success for me, for which I'll always be grateful. And it's led me down other paths, which have been truly rewarding. For example, since the Olympics I've taken on lots of roles that have helped me give something back and encourage individuals to get the most out of themselves.

After retiring from athletics at the end of 2005, I was awarded the role of National School Sport Champion, which I held for three years. (I had a great interest in young people doing sport, and I was also concerned about what kids were actually doing in terms of PE at school.) The job became a Government-backed role, supported by Norwich Union (now Aviva), and basically involved my working on ideas to get more kids doing more sport. Telling the then-Prime Minister, Gordon Brown, (on his second day in office) what I thought needed to be done was a weird experience – but what an opportunity. During those years, the UK Government target of getting 85 per cent of children doing at least two hours PE a week was realised (up from 25 per cent in 2002 – pretty good going!). I was so proud of that role and I'm glad I was able to inspire and motivate young people into a more active lifestyle – particularly those hardest to encourage: teenage girls, who often shy away from PE. In fact, the GirlsActive initiative (which I launched in 2006) was very much aimed at disengaged teenage girls. I found it shocking and disheartening to think that many girls have such low self-esteem or lack of confidence – whether as a result of peer pressure or because of body image issues.

In that role I ended up meeting young girls from all walks of life – including some who clearly didn't want to be there at all! (Teenagers do get a lot of bad press these days, but I suppose you could see why judging by the attitude of some of the girls that came through the door!) But I tell you, all the girls we met were great kids deep down, and clearly just needed someone who would listen to and believe in them. Some probably get in with the wrong crowd and others admitted they lacked structure in their home life generally. But despite all that, I believe they all had a hidden talent. (I just hope that, in time, they come to believe that themselves.) My aim was to get them interested in sports or activities, and to bring out those all-important qualities such as teamwork, self-belief, leadership, discipline, camaraderie and learning how to communicate – all the skills that sport itself helps to develop, and which you need in life. And I also wanted to tackle some of those body image issues. (Because, let's face it, if getting fitter makes you feel better about yourself and your body, then it's probably worth doing something active.)

I can't tell you how satisfying it has been seeing disengaged, unmotivated kids with their finger on the self-destruct button go from, 'I don't want to' and 'I can't,' to 'I can – and I want to...!' or at least 'I'm going to try!'

Mentoring people, especially up-and-coming young athletes is really important to me, too. It just occurred to me one day back in January 2004 that my experience as an athlete – all those setbacks, successes and disappointments – could help guide other young athletes through their own careers.

Mine was a real emotional and rocky ride – an athletics career often is – and young people need all the guidance they can get. So 'On Camp with Kelly' is my own mentoring and educational development programme funded by Aviva that aims to help junior international athletes reach their full potential. Seven years on I have supported and guided over 50 elite junior international standard athletes through their careers, and have seen them going through the big changes of life – physiological, social and emotional – such as leaving school and home, going to university or finding jobs – living as normal teenagers but with exceptional talents.

The initiative has been able to provide ongoing medical support and information, which has been so important, rehabilitation training and guidance, coaching support and one-to-one advice. My team and I are also here to give the girls support through any difficulties they may face – due to performance issues or educational demands, for example. At some stage they have all had injuries and some have had real downtimes to battle through, too, and I know they have all really benefitted from the additional support. With this support behind them, I hope these girls can at least go through their athletics careers saying they have given it their all. It's been really exciting and rewarding to know I've been part of their journey and to have seen them grow into respectable, talented young women. So watch this space! Maybe one day they will be writing a book too!

Helping people believe in themselves and find a purpose in life is one of the reasons I launched my own charity, The Dame Kelly Holmes Legacy Trust, **www.dkhlegacytrust.org**. I'm fully aware of the significant influence that someone like me – an elite athlete who has been there and done it – can have over young people.

We make the most of the talents of retired sports-people, and harness their expertise as they make the transition into new careers working within sport and education. I think people forget that sportspeople are all human – we just found our talent and made the most of it! Sportspeople come from a range of different backgrounds and take very different routes to success (mine certainly wasn't all plain sailing).

But what we tend to have in common is an ability to relate to kids and really get through to them. So in the 'Get on Track' programme, the sportspeople use their talents and abilities to help mentor disadvantaged young people. The kids on this programme have not had the best start in life, and they need guidance and intensive personal development before they can even be fit for employment and acquire the necessary social skills to get a job.

So yes, there's a lot in my life to keep me busy – and I still have plenty of other goals, too. I'm always looking for another challenge, a new career, a new path, something to get me out of bed in the morning, to put that fire back in my belly. All of which makes me just like so many of you out there.

So, what's next for me? Well, it's to make my mark in the business world – I'd like to set up my own business, from scratch, and watch it grow. I want to create something I can call my own, using my own ideas, my own hard work. I have a million and one ideas; I have needed to refine them, do my research, meet the right people. Then it's just about getting started.

Many people have dreams – to start their own business and be their own boss. For other people, the 'big goal' is to leave a job that no longer makes them happy, to take the plunge and find a new one somewhere else. Or change careers entirely. For a lot of people it may be to lose the weight that has made them unhappy for years. Or perhaps it's to run a marathon, or just to get a bit fitter, little by little. However big or small, these are challenges that require hard work, commitment and a belief in yourself that you can do it. And yes, it's a frightening thought and definitely not easy.

I have to say I well up with tears when I see the emotion on people's faces after they have achieved something they've been striving for. It doesn't have to be a massive accomplishment – but it's clearly a passionate desire, a huge goal to them. Losing just a few pounds, or toning up and actually liking their body again after years of struggle. Or getting round a fun run without collapsing. Finding out they're good at something when they thought they had no talent. You can just see that sense of triumph on people's faces. There's no feeling like it. It takes me back to my own life and reminds me of the hard work I had to put in and the overwhelming feeling of success ...

I remember – and understand – the rollercoaster ride it can often be to follow a dream. It can be exhausting, scary, time-consuming and really painful at times. But it's so worth all of that when that one thing finally comes to fruition.

I know I was lucky: I had a talent to run, but I also knew what I wanted. Not everyone does, they just know that what they have isn't quite enough to fulfil them. For those people, the hardest part is probably answering that first question: what is going to make me happy?

What's more, I know that plenty of people don't have that innate determination or insatiable drive. It's not in their make-up, so for them taking that step is much harder. But it's not impossible. And the rewards may be even greater when you reach your own target.

That's why I'm writing this book. I understand the quest for success and to feel good about yourself. I've been on a massive journey myself, and now that my Olympic dream is behind me, I feel I'm on another one. My career in the Army definitely shaped me when I was younger. Now I am older, there are different challenges ahead, but I really feel I am ready to make the most of what life offers now.

I'm aware that my experiences as an athlete have given me some valuable tools to guide others on their path. I understand what it's like to have to make changes to the pathway you thought you were on, taking tiny steps and having patience, and having to work really hard on your self-belief when you lose confidence in your ability. I did it every day. I know how easy it can be to talk yourself out of something before you actually get started. But I also know how to dig deep, summon that willpower and find the guts and determination to break through the barriers.

I believe everyone has a talent for something, and some have a unique ability. For me it was to run, and I'm lucky that my talent was clear enough to propel me to great things. Sometimes a person's gifts may not be so obvious, but that doesn't mean we can't all develop our skills. It frustrates me to see people waste their lives dreaming of changing something but never getting on and doing it because they (mistakenly) believe they're just not sufficiently talented or capable of achieving anything, feeling there are too many barriers in the way. My attitude is 'just go for it!' Even if it doesn't work out, or it takes longer than you thought or is much harder than you thought – at least you've given it a shot. What's crucial is to make sure your dream or aspiration is realistic – that way when you reach each little milestone along the way, it keeps you motivated.

I am not a psychologist or doctor, but I am a high achiever and love passing on my advice to help other people succeed. So, for everyone out there who, like me, never wants to live with 'if onlys ...', let's get started!

'*We would accomplish many more things if we did not think of them as impossible. A dream is not impossible so go get yours!*'

– Kelly

CHAPTER 1

Setting Goals (Ones You're Really Going to Reach)

'*Start with the big question: what do I want? Then ask yourself: what do I need to do to get there?' Be specific, break it down, and always keep it real.*'

– *Kelly*

So why don't we get down to basics. What do you really want from your life? OK, that may be the million-dollar question that keeps everyone up at night. Let's start instead by asking, 'Why are you reading this book?' Could it be you're thinking about a change in career? Are you planning to start a fitness regime? Do you want to be more successful in the career you're in? Do you just want to get your life more organised? Do you want to feel a bit happier and more fulfilled?

You may be sitting there knowing precisely what you want. You may not have a clue. Either way, you'll need to start by asking yourself some fundamental questions.

One of my coaches, the late Dave Arnold, asked me quite early on in my running career, 'Are you in it for the medals or the money?' This was in about 1994, after I had run in the semi-final of the World Championships the year before – coming fifth – and I had set a new

English record for the 800m of 1:58.64. Athens was still a long way off then, but already I was competing with the very best, and on my way to bigger things.

It was a great question to put to an athlete – or to anyone really. A good way to learn where your priorities lie. (Although being in the Army definitely kept my feet on the ground anyway.)

I didn't hesitate for a minute: 'Medals,' I answered. For me, the driving force was the sense of elation and achievement when all your hard work and training have paid off. For that huge buzz when you cross the line. That fantastic sense of victory when you win ... Yes, my motives were crystal clear to me.

To be honest, I had always been equally focused about my choice of career. From the age of 14 I had wanted to join the British Army and get a job as a physical training instructor (PTI). I have always been single-minded when I want something; I go there to get it and fight for it. And if there is a knock-back I try again – like the Japanese proverb says, 'Get knocked down seven times, stand up eight.' I had seven years of bad injuries. And then in the eighth year I won my two gold medals.

So from my teens until I was 35 I always knew what I wanted – in terms of big life goals, that is. But I know that not everyone is so sure about where they want to be. Some of my friends find it tough, and I meet people every day who say they don't have a clue. They drift along hoping they'll bump into it one day and wondering what life has in store.

If you're one of those people, it's time to get thinking – because if you really, really want something, and keep a sense of reality about what it is you want, chances are you probably can get there. You may just need certain skills to help you along the way.

I have learned some important lessons in my life, and over the years have acquired some fundamental skills that I feel everyone can use to get what they want. I believe there is a set of key stepping stones, call it a kind of formula, which, if followed with focus and commitment, can help you along that path to success. You can break them down, and that's what I've done in this book. They go something like this:

1. Set yourself a goal (making sure it's realistic)
2. Be organised (plan, prepare, execute)
3. Think positive (start believing you can do it)
4. Learn to overcome obstacles (all-important strategies to help you through the tough times)
5. Stay motivated (work on your willpower)
6. Enjoy the journey (very important, this one)

They're not hard-and-fast rules, but they're the basic principles you need – and I needed – to reach success.

The secret, too, is to really get to know yourself – and the best way to do that is to keep thinking, asking yourself questions and writing it all down – your thoughts, your targets, any inspiring words from the successful and famous (or ordinary and not-famous, but wise), anything that helps you. And always keep that inner dialogue going – What do I want? Am I prepared? How am I going to get there? Am I getting there? And, importantly: am I enjoying it?

WHAT DO I WANT?

I dreamed of Olympic glory when I was 14 – it was 1984 and I had watched Sebastian Coe win gold in the 1,500 metres in Los Angeles. It was, of course, back then, pure fantasy. A sort of, 'Wouldn't that be amazing?' daydream. I said to myself, 'One day I want to be Olympic champion.' But who'd have known it would come true? The very first step, then, is to try answering that million-dollar question: what is it I want? Only you can answer this one. So the first exercise is to get a clean piece of paper and start writing down some ideas. Think sky blue – dare to fantasise.

These following five questions should help you explore this big issue in more depth. Take your initial thoughts and break them down further by working on your answers to these:

1. What Matters to Me?

- What is most important to me?
- Wealth?
- Independence?
- A better work/life balance?
- Seeing the world?
- Getting out of debt?
- Feeling stronger and healthier?

2. What Makes Me Happy?

- What has made me happy in the past?
- What do I most enjoy doing?
- How would I spend my time if I didn't have to do the job I do now?
- What gives me most pleasure in life?
- If I won the lottery tomorrow, how would I spend my days?

It might help to shift the question and ask:

- What makes me unhappy?
- What do I most want to change about where I am now?

3. What Am I Good At?

Here's where it's useful to list your talents. Again, list anything you can think of:

- What are my strengths?
- What do I know about?
- What are my talents?
- What would I describe as my glories?
- What are my greatest achievements (even small ones count)?

Doing this can help you work out which direction you should be heading in – in your career, for example.

4. Who Inspires Me?

And why? This can be someone incredibly famous, or it can be someone who lives down the road. But try to get away from fantasising about reality TV stars who have made lots of money by chance. Think about someone whose qualities you really admire, a man or woman who has achieved great things through sheer hard work and passion, someone whose achievements you would like to emulate in some way.

5. Where Would I Like to Be?

Where would you like to be in six months or a year's time? In two and five years' time? Again, try to keep this within the realms of reality. Winning the lottery or being a supermodel probably aren't ... being a stone lighter, or in a new career, or even doing your first triathlon just might be. What can you honestly see yourself achieving some months, or years, down the line?

Be Careful What You Wish For...

Your goals don't have to be about material success, fame or fortune. Personal growth goals are incredibly important, too; in fact, one study of college students published in the *Journal of Research in Personality* found that working on your inner self – setting goals that involve increasing your confidence, your health and emotional well-being, your friendships and relationships, for example – is the real key to finding happiness. In the study, the students who spent two years after graduating pursuing these kinds of 'personal' goals – such as working on friendships, or their health and personal inner success, or getting involved in their communities – were actually happier than those who spent those two years pursuing material goals such as wealth and fame and looks. Setting and focusing on goals that achieve greater happiness and emotional well-being is more likely to bring you lasting rewards.

So, are you any closer yet to finding a direction? This kind of soul searching might be really difficult, but it's a vital way to get started.

A few years ago I met a young girl who seemed to have no enthusiasm, no dreams for the future whatsoever. We met when her school visited an outward bound centre as part of my GirlsActive initiative.

She clearly didn't want to be there, and had been bad-mouthing and swearing at some of our team members – all earrings and attitude, with that kind of 'I'd rather be anywhere but here' and 'I don't give a damn' look on her face. Picture your stereotypical teenager who hasn't had anyone in her life to encourage or motivate her – that's what she was like; there wasn't a glimpse of enthusiasm within her, just a desire to be destructive and negative.

I decided to spend a lot of time with her that day, desperate to find within her some kind of hope for the future or positive reaction to what life held for her. We talked and talked – I'd match each one of her (many) negatives with a positive; in fact I started mirroring her slang just to be able to communicate – but then, little by little, she started to relax, look at me, and talk instead of groan.

And then, finally, a breakthrough. She said she did like the idea of having a career, and that she really wanted to work in childcare. We talked about how that could come about, what she'd need to do to get there. As we broke it down into small, achievable steps – getting the information, talking to the right people, applying to the right colleges – it suddenly became clear to her that this actually was within her reach. That, despite what she had been led to believe to this point, she could be good at something – that she was perfectly able to forge her own career and path in life. The change in her was amazing, instant – you could see it on her face. Like a light going on. That transformation from 'there's nothing for me' to, 'hey, I could do that.' It was the look of hope, I suppose.

For those who already have a direction – 'I want to get fit,' 'I want to change my career,' 'I want to move to the country and work for myself' – then you're ready to start with step number one. Here's where you sit down and set yourself a really specific, concrete plan, along with a set of smaller goals to help turn that dream into reality.

Write It Down

One US study looked at a group of students who graduated from Yale – of whom 3 per cent had written down specific goals about what they wanted to achieve later in life. When they were surveyed years later, the results showed that the ones who had written down their goals had not only achieved their goals, they were also worth more financially than the other 97 per cent!

SETTING GOALS

What's the Difference between a Dream and a Goal?

This is how I see it: if the dream is the big picture, goals are grounded in reality; they're the specific steps you take along the way. Dreams are great – they're the springboard to change. But you need to shape your goals, break them down into achievable targets, and then into even smaller ones still.

For example, you may dream of being super-fit and having a really great, toned body. For some, that could translate into a big specific goal such as running a half marathon, or losing 20lb. As goals, these in turn have to be broken into smaller short-term targets – monthly, weekly and daily – that incorporate the steps you need to take to get there. It might help to create a flowchart or action plan. Write down the big goal in the middle, e.g. 'get fit – run my first 5k race' – with lots of arrows showing the necessary components to get there (see following pages for examples).

QUIZ: ARE YOU READY FOR CHANGE?

Sometimes we're not sure what we want, and many of us have times when we doubt our ability to create change at all (we'll deal with this self-doubt more thoroughly in Chapter 3). To help you focus on where you want to go, here's something to get you thinking. Think about three good things that have happened in your life. For each one, ask yourself:

1) What role did I play in influencing this situation?

2) Which aspects of this good thing were driven by me, and which were out of my control?

Thinking about the positive contribution you have made to the successes in your life so far can help remind you that you're capable of realising another goal – and doing it well!

When I think back to my first big goal in life, I realise it had nothing to do with running. It wasn't to win

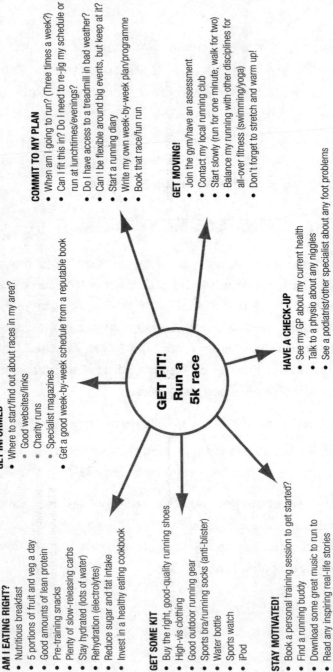

AM I EATING RIGHT?
- Nutritious breakfast
- 5 portions of fruit and veg a day
- Good amounts of lean protein
- Pre-training snacks
- Plenty of slow-releasing carbs
- Stay hydrated (lots of water)
- Rehydration (electrolytes)
- Reduce sugar and fat intake
- Invest in a healthy eating cookbook

GET SOME KIT
- Buy the right, good-quality running shoes
- High-vis clothing
- Good outdoor running gear
- Sports bra/running socks (anti-blister)
- Water bottle
- Sports watch
- iPod

STAY MOTIVATED!
- Book a personal training session to get started?
- Find a running buddy
- Download some great music to run to
- Read any inspiring real-life stories
- Write down my reasons for wanting to do this (pin them up!)

GET INFORMED
- Where to start/find out about races in my area?
  - Good websites/links
  - Charity runs
  - Specialist magazines
- Get a good week-by-week schedule from a reputable book

GET FIT!
Run a
5k race

HAVE A CHECK-UP
- See my GP about my current health
- Talk to a physio about any niggles
- See a podiatrist/other specialist about any foot problems
- Find out if there is a good local sports massage therapist

COMMIT TO MY PLAN
- When am I going to run? (Three times a week?)
- Can I fit this in? Do I need to re-jig my schedule or run at lunchtimes/evenings?
- Do I have access to a treadmill in bad weather?
- Can I be flexible around big events, but keep at it?
- Start a running diary
- Write my own week-by-week plan/programme
- Book that race/fun run

GET MOVING!
- Join the gym/have an assessment
- Contact my local running club
- Start slowly (run for one minute, walk for two)
- Balance my running with other disciplines for all-over fitness (swimming/yoga)
- Don't forget to stretch and warm up!

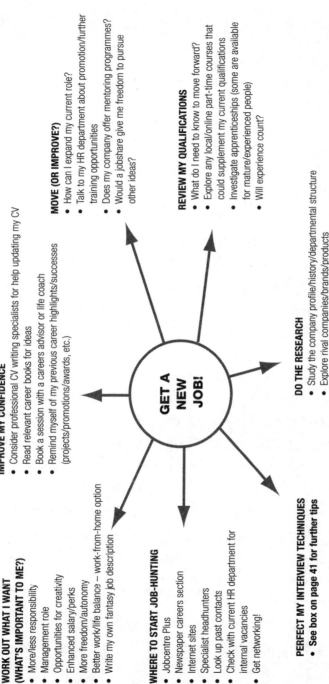

WORK OUT WHAT I WANT (WHAT'S IMPORTANT TO ME?)
- More/less responsibility
- Management role
- Opportunities for creativity
- Enhanced salary/perks
- More freedom/autonomy
- Better work/life balance – work-from-home option
- Write my own fantasy job description

IMPROVE MY CONFIDENCE
- Consider professional CV writing specialists for help updating my CV
- Read relevant career books for ideas
- Book a session with a careers advisor or life coach
- Remind myself of my previous career highlights/successes (projects/promotions/awards, etc.)

MOVE (OR IMPROVE?)
- How can I expand my current role?
- Talk to my HR department about promotion/further training opportunities
- Does my company offer mentoring programmes?
- Would a jobshare give me freedom to pursue other ideas?

REVIEW MY QUALIFICATIONS
- What do I need to know to move forward?
- Explore any local/online part-time courses that could supplement my current qualifications
- Investigate apprenticeships (some are available for mature/experienced people)
- Will experience count?

GET A NEW JOB!

DO THE RESEARCH
- Study the company profile/history/departmental structure
- Explore rival companies/brands/products
- What's the market doing?
- Which companies impress me and why?

WHERE TO START JOB-HUNTING
- Jobcentre Plus
- Newspaper careers section
- Internet sites
- Specialist headhunters
- Look up past contacts
- Check with current HR department for internal vacancies
- Get networking!

PERFECT MY INTERVIEW TECHNIQUES
- **See box on page 41 for further tips**

an Olympic medal. It was actually to buy my parents a tumble dryer – which I intended to do on my own, with my own money, which I would earn myself. And I can honestly say achieving it taught me important lessons about how to set yourself a goal and realise that you can achieve it if you put your mind to it.

We had very little money as a family, so a tumble dryer was considered a true luxury. I knew that having one would save my mum so much time and energy, so I decided I'd buy her and my stepdad Mick our own machine for Christmas – for the princely sum of £129. Back then, in the early 1980s, that was a ton of money, especially for a kid. The only way I was ever going to get that kind of money was to work for it. Work? Well, do more on my weekly paper rounds, which paid me £12 a week. I did all the sums (which wasn't my forte!) and calculated that by putting aside £10 a week, which I gave my granddad so he could drive down to Currys on a Friday, I'd be only £30 short by Christmas. To cover the shortfall I knew I needed to supplement my income – which I decided to do by washing my neighbours' windows or cars – at about £5 a car (but boy did I do a good job before I got paid!). The look on my mum's and Mick's faces – a real picture of shock, pride, gratitude and pure pleasure as Mum undid the massive ribbon I'd tied around the machine – was worth it. Worth all my efforts, the planning, the secrecy, the military operation of getting the tumble dryer on a wheelbarrow from my nan and grandad's next door and trying not to drop it, the trudging round the streets delivering papers in all weathers. What it also gave me was an awareness of my own power to achieve what I wanted, if I really wanted it.

I had big athletics goals, too, though, even as a teenager. Once it became obvious – when I was 12 – that I had this ability to run, it was really exciting. I started running competitively in the winter of '82, and by the summer of '83 I had won my first major title – English Schools Champion at 1,500m. Even at that early age I realised I hated losing and that I had a voice inside me saying 'I want to win.' I knew there were people better than me, who might train harder than me, but I also realised that I could beat them if I trained harder myself, and worked on the areas I might be weak on.

After winning that schools event in '83, my big goal was to win it for a second year. It didn't go to plan that time – I didn't win – but even at 13 and 14 I was learning the lesson that in order to win on the track, you have to follow a plan. I had to have a training schedule devised by my coach. And at 14, when my friends were out playing or meeting up, going to clubs and listening to music (in fact, just being teenagers), I had this weekly schedule of training. I'd train three to four times a week – on top of which I'd bike to school (three miles) and back. I'd meet my coach in the afternoon for training after school, then bike back home afterwards. It all became part of the routine.

I suppose I was that kind of child – determined, resourceful, a go-getter. Although academically I didn't excel at all (schoolwork didn't come naturally to me, and I spent a lot of the time wishing I wasn't there; in fact I saw more corridors than classrooms), I still realised early on that if you want something in life you need a plan and a timeline. And a real will to get there.

Yes, having *the will* helps. I remember being completely unshakeable in my decision to have a career in the Army when I left school. I nagged my mum to take me to the Army careers office when I was 15, even though we were sent away and told to come back when I was 17 and 9 months (the recruitment age at that time). But each year I'd make her take me over to the Army careers office, just in case they'd lowered the entry age! I couldn't wait to get started. And when I did finally reach the right age, and pass the entry requirements, I was gutted to find out that my dream job – being a PT instructor – wasn't available as all the courses were full up. So instead I took the next best thing on offer (being an

HGV driver), and from then on started planning my route to getting the PT job I'd always been after. (It wasn't an easy path, but more of that later.)

Any athlete will tell you that this kind of goal-setting is key to success. From year to year you know what your main targets are – for example, every year for an athlete there are major championships such as the Commonwealth Games, European Championships, World Championships and the Olympic Games – and you work backwards from those to the here-and-now. During a year you may need to run 10 or 12 grand prix races. And you also need to run the trials in order to achieve the time and placing to make the selection. So you have lots of different targets all leading to that end goal – the big championship.

It doesn't stop there. For example, you have different phases of training in the winter – longer, more endurance-based runs, as well as strength training. Your summer training plan will be more intense, faster, with specific track sessions.

My coach used to give me a schedule of what we planned to do that week – what day, what time and where. Depending on the time of year, this would be a mixture of circuits, weight training, hill running, speed work on the track and so on. Included in the plan would be warm-up and warm-down periods, stretching, physiotherapy visits, massages, nutritional plan, ice baths, catnaps and a good sleep routine.

And I'd know, each week, exactly what my schedule was. Of course, sometimes you'd have to adjust – like anything in life. You might get a niggle or a cold, so you'd have to rework your plan, but the plan was your focal point. At the back of your mind you would keep that big goal – the Olympics or other championships, but in the shorter term you'd focus on those smaller targets – such as a certain time you'd have to reach in a race, or recovery rate you'd aim to meet in order to move on to the next repetition or stage of training. Everything is target-orientated when you're an athlete.

So let's see how this could work for you. The best way to make sure your goal has a successful outcome is to ensure it's a SMART goal. This is a well-known acronym used by businesses and development experts around the world. Your goal has to be:

Specific

It has to be precise and really clear. So, something general such as 'I want to tone up' is not clear. Instead you need to aim for something like, 'I'd like to look slimmer by losing 5lb by 15th June, so I can get into that outfit for that wedding.' Another non-specific goal would be 'I want to get out of the job I hate.' Instead, you need to set it down as, 'I want to be in a new job that I love in 6 months' time.' Remember, there has to be an end point to your goal or it can go on forever with no focus.

Once you have the bigger aspiration, then you can start working on the plan. So instead of vague intentions (e.g. 'I want to get more qualifications'), decide, 'I want to get an Open University degree in Maths by 2012.'

Measurable

This is where you give yourself a frame of reference. This helps you know exactly where you're going – because you've been really clear about when you'll know you've succeeded. So how will you know you've achieved your goal? The end point may be actually starting that job, or running that race, or achieving that specific turnover target for your new business. Think in concrete terms – times, dates, amounts. If you're trying to get out of debt, for example, or save money, you need to specify an amount of money. Only once you have made a measurable achievement will you know it's time to celebrate that ultimate success.

Attainable

It's really important to make sure the goal you're setting for yourself is achievable. Do you really have the commitment and enthusiasm for it? Your goal can be aspirational, of course, but if you're not being honest with yourself about your abilities you're not likely to get there. And, what's worse, it will really dent your confidence for other goals. Don't aim to win that first triathlon you're aiming to do, but tell yourself you'll come in the first half of the field – or actually finish it! Making a million in your first year of starting your new business may be pitching too high! Be ambitious, of course, but also remember you need to feel confident that you can get there.

Realistic

In a nutshell, this means 'Are you living in the real world?' Do you have the resources – time, money and skills – to realise this goal? If you're giving up your job to set up your own business, do you have enough savings to live on? Can you realistically finance your project? Are you physically able to commit the time to all the study you will need to do to pass your degree? Make sure you keep your feet firmly in reality when planning your goal.

Time-Framed

This is all about times and dates. Here's where you give yourself a start date and a completion point – 'I'll start my weight-management programme on Monday, and I'm aiming to lose that 7lb by my summer holiday.' Don't forget to break it up into small weekly or monthly targets, too – this helps keep you motivated. It could be something like, 'Every Tuesday, Thursday and Saturday I'll aim to do 40 minutes of vigorous exercise.' Framing your goal this way gives you all-important deadlines, which also gives you a sense of urgency.

The Science of Step by Step

Turning your big goal into a set of small tasks that you can tick off, one at a time, is far more effective than thinking about it in abstract terms, according to research published in the journal *Psychological Science*. In a study, people were asked to break their goal down into the possible steps involved. The researchers found that people who took this approach – detail by detail – made more progress on an assigned task, and also got an earlier start on it, than people who thought about the task in abstract, more general terms.

Write down your goal: Keep it on the fridge, in your wallet, on your bedroom wall so it's staring at you when you wake up in the morning! Just make sure it's visible – it helps you stay on track and remain focused.

TRY THIS!

It helps to write down *why* you want to achieve that goal. Ask yourself, why is this so important to me? Sit down and start to think about all the reasons you may have for setting yourself this particular goal. What's the motivating force or forces? What do you think it can bring you – confidence, cash, a creative outlet? Think of all the reasons you are setting yourself this particular goal – 'I want to run 5km because it will help me lose weight/so that I can raise money for charity/so that I can look great in that new outfit in time for that holiday next summer/because getting fitter will help me feel happier/for that huge sense of self-esteem when I've crossed the line,' etc. Everything you write down is another reason to get going, and stay focused. Think of it as a kind of checklist. Even while you're pursuing your main goal, you'll probably find you are realising some of those smaller aims.

BE FLEXIBLE

One of the most important lessons to learn about successful goal-setting is when to change tack or re-evaluate the goal. Life doesn't always go to plan. As an athlete you have carefully made plans written in a training diary. As the saying goes, Life is a roller-coaster, you've just got to ride it. You write down how each training session went, such as what the weather was like, or how you felt that day.

Everyone will have times when they just can't stick to their weekly plan – just like an athlete. Sometimes an athlete might have to miss certain training sessions because of work commitments, or they are ill or injured, or a train or flight is cancelled. The truth is there are outside influences that affect even the most carefully prepared plan.

I've had to abandon many original schedules due to injury. For example, my training in 2000 started really badly: from 3rd January I had the journey from hell with injury. On 21st January my glands came up and I had to pull out of a race. Less than two weeks after I started training I got injured again: I slipped in a cross country race and damaged my right leg, losing the sensation in it for three months. This led to over two months of no running and limited training. The emotional impact was terrible. I was down, I cried, I was in pain – and it was 2000 (an Olympic year), so I had a massive goal. That year my training was a rollercoaster ride with mountains to climb and some steep, fierce descents! Injury upon injury intermingled with some good training sessions. I could have given up. But I didn't. Instead my coach and I had to constantly reassess the various targets and completely adapt my training by finding other methods to try to keep fit. And I had to somehow keep smiling. (I won the Bronze Medal in the 800 metres at the Olympic Games, and was a finalist in the 1,500 metres, so it wasn't all bad!) That was a tough year but with perseverence I still achieved a lot.

So yes, having targets is really important, but it's equally important to realise that along the way, something may interfere with them – something beyond your control. That's when you have to say, 'OK, how do I address it?,' 'Maybe that target was too high,' 'Maybe I focused too much on one area.' These things are always worth evaluating.

And when it goes really well, ask yourself, 'Should I be stepping up to the next level?' If it didn't go to plan, ask *why* it didn't. (We'll look at this more in Chapter 4.)

The bottom line is, have a vision, set that goal, break it down, make those plans, have a vision – but remind yourself it's OK to adapt this along the way, or even re-evaluate the goal altogether if you find there's a different, better direction out there for you.

Notes from my diary:

'As long as you believe in yourself you can achieve anything' – 12th Sept 2000

'Inspired to go all the way!' – 20th Sept 2000

'Gobsmacked and overwhelmed!' – 26th Sept 2000, after getting the Bronze Medal in the 800m at the Sydney Olympics

WHAT TO DO TODAY FOR SUCCESS TOMORROW

✓ *Ask yourself those all-important questions to help you focus on what you want out of life.* Write it all down. Use the answers to help you zero in on your one big goal.

✓ *OK, have you got a goal in mind? Now write yourself an action plan or a goal 'flowchart'.* What do you need to do to help realise that goal? It's a step-by-step process, remember, so break it up into bite-sized chunks

✓ *Set daily goals.* Ask yourself, 'What can I do today to help me reach my ultimate aim? What does success look like to me?' A daily goal can be easily achieved, and it's really motivating when you can tick it off. It means you've climbed another rung on the ladder, or gone another mile on the road to success.

✓ *Visualise yourself reaching your goal.* Believe you can do it. Spend five minutes each day – in the morning, and as you go to bed at night – visualising yourself succeeding.

✓ *Keep notes along the way* – one day you will look back and see where you came from.

CHAPTER 2

Getting Organised: Fast-track Success with the Right Preparation

'Being organised means making your own rules, your own timelines, and being clear about your priorities. It's about taking control.'

– Kelly

Athens. Summer 2004. The night before the 1,500 metres final. Slowly, calmly, I started getting ready – carefully laying everything I would need for the next day's race on a chair.

As always, there was a place for everything – my bag, bottles with my carbohydrate and protein drinks prepared, shorts, crop top with my race numbers pinned on it (I always made sure I had eight pins and that they were put into the number across the corner). My t-shirt and tracksuit (laid out in order of bottoms and tops), socks, trainers and spikes (racing shoes) were put on the floor by the chair. It was a ritual I had performed at every race and at every championship in my career, in whatever country that might be and whichever hotel room. Having my kit where I could see it was always incredibly important to me; it was my way of getting completely focused and ready for what lay ahead.

It helped me most of the time – it gave me confidence, and was, in a way, the finishing touch to my preparation.

It made me feel ready to perform ...

JUGGLING TRICKS

But I have to be honest with you. I'm not always completely organised. You can't always describe my home as calm, or streamlined. I have 20 things on my to-do list (that's just today), my emails are piling up at a scary rate, and sometimes there are about three suitcases backed up by the front door from all the trips I've recently come back from – and I just haven't had time to unpack them. My hallway looks like an airport baggage lounge half the time!

I really do think we should at least aim to stay organised, though. Being organised filters down through the rest of life. I know that my life certainly flows better when everything's in order. Plus I get incredibly frustrated when my environment is untidy.

The truth is, many of us find it a real struggle to juggle work and home, let alone squeezing in outside interests and hobbies. And, since retiring from athletics (when my daily schedule, out of necessity, was carefully planned and organised), I have found that my new work life often gets crazy! I'm involved with so many projects and charities, it's just not possible to keep on top of absolutely everything. Often I'm just running in and out of my house like a mad woman. Sometimes I just come home to sleep – I get off a plane, come home, drop that suitcase, go to bed, get up, pack another bag, head out the door. Again and again ...

There's so much stuff in my head at any one time – all the people I have to call, my mentoring projects and charity work to organise, appearances to make, boards to sit on. Then there are contracts to work on, ideas to flesh out, emails to respond to, papers to sign and fan mail to reply to.

Don't get me wrong, I do love the challenge. And I'm lucky that I have a great team to help me stay on top of things. But sometimes it gets a bit overwhelming. And it frustrates me that all this clutter – all the stuff in my head, those endless things on my to-do list, all the piles of paperwork – that all this is preventing me from forging ahead on some of the next goals I've set for myself.

So I'm certainly not holier than thou about being organised all the time. But if there's one essential lesson I learned during my athletics career and my years in the Army, it's the importance of being prepared and getting organised if you want achieve and move forward.

That's why, when it all gets too much – the clutter around me and those to-do lists that keep getting longer – I get into 'the zone'. I say to myself, 'OK, it's time to take action. Enough is enough.' Then I take a step back and work out what needs to be done.

I start chucking things out, sifting through my email inbox, prioritising my to-do lists, delegating where I can, unpacking those suitcases – having a massive sort-out until it gets done and I feel I'm back on track again. It may take a while. But I get there and it feels great.

So let's think about why preparation and organisation can help you be more successful. How can being prepared and organised help you achieve that life-changing goal you've set for yourself?

Here's how I see it.

WHY GET ORGANISED?

First, being organised makes you feel clear-headed, in control, confident, efficient. We all know how clutter, lack of clear time-keeping and not being properly prepared can make you feel stressed and inefficient. You can't think clearly, you can't find your keys or that vital document, you forget to call people back, you miss appointments or you double-book yourself, or you can't pull out that important email amidst the pile of junk emails. You get behind, you miss opportunities. You may get in a mess with your finances, or just become incredibly stressed, which affects your health. You could even end up not following your dream because you just can't find the time to do it, because you've taken so much on. Perhaps you just end up rushing from A to B, not really enjoying any of it. Life becomes out of control. There's no real plan, no structure. It's that feeling that you get when it's all taking over. A bit like drowning. I have experienced all these feelings and it doesn't feel good.

Now think back to that goal you may have set yourself in Chapter 1. To achieve that goal, having a plan – step by step – is absolutely vital. And the bottom line is it'll be so much easier to follow that plan if you know everything else in your life feels like it's on track.

Make sure you know you have time to follow each stage of your goal, that you have the energy and motivation to get you there. Think about it: if you're going to succeed at that Open University degree, you need to know you can factor in the time to fill in the application, but also to know you have allocated slots in your life to ensure you're able to study and keep up to date with your essays and assignments.

And if you've decided you want to change your career, you need to be able to research other fields, get to know the job market, work on your CV and prepare for those interviews.

To succeed you need to know what you're talking about, look the part, be able to impress and project your most efficient, confident self.

So being 'organised' is more than having a bit of a tidy up – it's about freeing up important time, taking a holistic approach to your new life direction, which involves tightening up your life *right now* to secure that bigger picture.

So, am I saying you need to have a house free of clutter to lose those 10lb? Of course not. But what I do believe is that your environment can have a big impact on your feelings of well-being. In a clear and clean environment you're more likely to feel clear-headed and energetic. You often feel you're stagnating when you're bogged down by piles of stuff and household mess. I certainly find that a new goal or project is easier to pursue when I've cleared the decks, made some concrete written plans, perhaps rejigged my diary, taken steps that allow me to factor those new plans into my life.

Say, for example, you want to lose 10lb. Perhaps overhauling your kitchen is a really good exercise to kickstart you? Chuck out all those out-of-date foods

WHAT'S YOUR GOAL? GETTING THE JOB YOU WANT

Performing well at that interview can make all the difference. Proper preparation means you'll have answers to the following questions at your fingertips:

- *Why do you want the job? What's your motivation?*

- *What skills might you have acquired in the past that you could bring to the job? Punctuality, communication skills, supporting people, managing situations, looking after money.*

- *Why are YOU the right person for the job? Personality, experience and how you cope with certain situations.*

- *Is your CV up-to-date? Is it clear and up-to-date? Does it reflect you and your key achievements?*

And don't forget:

- *presentation/appearance. What will you wear? Will you be groomed, smart, efficient-looking?*

- *bring things with you that demonstrate your ability (CV, previous projects/cuttings, etc.)*

- *have some questions prepared about the job/company/future direction of the business*

- *talk slowly and calmly*

- *perfect that firm handshake*

- *maintain eye contact – and smile!*

or tempting goodies, clear the cupboards for your healthy new lifestyle. Or reorganise your kitchen so that it inspires you to eat healthily – start looking at recipes, get some healthy eating books from the library or shop, cut out useful info you find in the paper. Put the fat fryer away, get out the steamer. Invest in a new fruit bowl, veg rack or smoothie maker. These are small, simple preparations – call them 'tweaks' to your environment – which can inspire you, make you feel you've taken that first step and are well on your way to achieving that goal. Or do the same to your wardrobe – anything that helps you to think ahead and start the ball rolling.

You could take the same approach to getting fit. You may need to take a look at all your current commitments – working and social – and streamline your diary around exercise classes. Do you need to get a check-up at the doctor's before you start? Do you have some good workout gear and the right trainers? Do you want to invest in a gym membership? Could you invest in a personal trainer? Do you need to get childcare or someone to walk the dog so you can make that Tuesday class? Have you got someone you can go with? What little changes can you make in your life today to help ensure you stay committed to your goal?

The hardest part is getting started.

GETTING ORGANISED

Get a pen and paper and sit down for 20 minutes or so to think about how organised your life is right now. Break it down into different areas – work, home, office, desk, finances – whatever applies to you.

The aim is to work out which areas of your life are most disorganised. And once you've identified them, think about in what ways they are out of control.

Then think about the goal you set for yourself in Chapter 1. Ask yourself, to what extent is this disorganisation holding me back from my goal? How does it make me feel? How much more successful would my life be if I were more organised? What would work better if certain areas of my life were more structured? What steps can I take to get more control in those areas?

Despite what I say about often feeling in a state of chaos these days, I do know *how* to sort things out. As I said, you can't be a successful athlete – or have a career in the Army – without acquiring some pretty effective organisation skills.

In the Army, everything is about discipline and structure. It gets drummed into you. When you're a new recruit you have to be prepared for regular inspections – of your kit or your bed, both of which have to be spick and span at all times.

I remember having to bull shine my parade shoes until they shone like glass. I spent so many evenings sitting in the corridors spitting on my cloth and rubbing black polish into those shoes – round and round in small, small circles until you could almost see your face in them. Shirts had to be pressed with absolute precision – creases in the sleeves had to be razor sharp, starched and stiff as a board! In the early days my badly ironed shirts were regularly flung on the floor, and one time my bed was tipped over because the blankets weren't piled exactly right.

When I was working as an Army physical training instructor (PTI), part of my role was to manage a gym as well as having to schedule dozens of classes and courses, not to mention learning the rules of loads of sports, and then passing these on to the soldiers. And of course I had to be on time, and stay on time. Equally, when you're on an Army exercise, everything is tightly scheduled and planned down to the last detail. They don't call it military precision for nothing!

Learning those organisational skills in the Army stood me in good stead for my career in elite athletics, where meticulous preparation is fundamental.

For a start, as an athlete you have to know when, *and* where, *and* how you're going to train – day in, day out, week in, week out, all year round. You need to know what to eat, when, what you should be doing after training – such as massage, physio, resting and so on. Most athletes work from written weekly schedules – you have to be aware at all times what you need to be doing when; that's how meticulously planned your life is.

Time management was always important as an athlete. If training was scheduled for, say, 10 a.m., then you would have to be there by 9:30 a.m. warmed up and ready to go at 10! The coach would be, and so you would have to be, too. You have to be constantly thinking ahead: what time is that flight I need to get to those championships? What time does my race start? When should I eat and sleep to help my body work most efficiently and be ready for that race? Is my kit ready? As an elite athlete, if you let anything slide you throw your training out of synch, which jeopardises your fitness levels, and in turn your ability to be as good as you need to be. It can lose you that race, that medal. It's as simple as that.

That's not to say there aren't occasions when it all goes wrong. We're only human. I remember an event in Gateshead in 2001 when I arrived at the meet without any kit. I'd been at an event in Zurich two days earlier and had flown back to the UK, only to realise my luggage hadn't! I'd stupidly forgotten to pack my spikes in my hand luggage – massive mistake for an athlete! Running shoes are very personal and crucial to the way you perform – arriving at an event without them was a nightmare! I wasn't racing until the afternoon, which meant I at least had some time to go shopping. I needed to find a certain brand of clothing, trainers and spikes (because of my sponsors), and spent hours going round Newcastle trying to find replacement kit. As a result I was exhausted, hadn't eaten properly, and missed my usual pre-race rest.

One hour before the race I still hadn't found any spikes. Can you imagine?

Before going looking for replacement kit I'd already checked with my friend and fellow athlete, 5,000-metre runner Jo Pavey, what size her feet were. Fortunately they were the same size as mine and her shoes the same make, so in the end I asked her if I could borrow her spikes, and she kindly agreed. The trouble was, her race was directly before mine. So there we were, madly swapping shoes – which were, by now, all hot and sweaty – as the other athletes were lining up for the 800 metres! Not the most professional approach!

Having said that, I ran a great race, and won it at 1:58.10 – which was also the fastest time I'd run that season, which earned me the award for Performance of the Meet! A happy ending to a very stressful event. I think the adrenaline kicked in and I didn't spend time getting anxious and nervous about the race. Still, a lesson well and truly learned in both respects.

So let's get organised. I've listed here the six key organisational 'tools' or golden rules I cannot live without, and that I recommend for everyone:

1 GET A DIARY

In many ways, a diary should be your number one piece of kit – it's absolutely critical. As an athlete you need it to plan and record your training to assess your progress, commenting in it how you felt afterwards, what you did in the session, your times and recovery. Or you list the factors that might have influenced your session – the weather, your emotions, what you ate, any health niggles, etc.

I always stress to the young athletes I am mentoring the importance of keeping a diary – it's *the* best way to get to know yourself as an athlete and to make progress. I tell them not to just rely on the coach or someone else to write all the details for them – they're not with you 24/7, and they won't write how you feel.

Even now I use a diary or a little black book for

my ideas, new projects, or fantasies that I believe I could turn into reality! It's invaluable.

So when you're starting out on your goal, get yourself a nice big, solid diary – in it you'll be writing down all your ideas, as well as that 'flowchart' of action we talked about in Chapter 1 that helps you work out how you're going to achieve your goal in small steps. Also record in your diary any thoughts, or tips, or cuttings, you come across along the way. Ditch all those scrappy bits of paper you scribble those ideas on. One diary is far more effective than loads of Post-it® notes that you'll only end up losing!

In your diary you can have a record of your whole journey, and it's incredibly motivating to look back and see how far you've come. A diary is also a really good way to offload when everything is getting on top of you. I know my diary has often given me somewhere to express my frustrations and anxiety – when I felt I couldn't express them to anyone else. (It's a good idea to use a separate diary for this – focus on positive energy in your main diary.)

Keeping a Diary Boosts Weight Loss

A diary can double your weight loss according to research published in the *American Journal of Preventive Medicine*. The more people wrote down and recorded what they ate, the more likely they were to succeed on their weight loss programme. In fact, people who kept daily food records lost twice as much weight as people who kept no records. It's thought that reflecting on our behaviour, keeping track of our habits – simply writing it all down – encourages us to consume fewer calories.

Other research has found that keeping a diary is good for your emotional health. Scientists from UCLA have found that keeping a diary – recording your thoughts and feelings – can reduce activity in the amygdala, the part of the brain which helps govern intensity of emotions, and therefore leave you happier.

2   BE CLEAR ABOUT PRIORITIES

The bottom line is, you can't work efficiently – in any field – if you're always chasing your tail. We're short on time as it is these days, and many of us have too many demands on us. This makes it really hard to devote the necessary time to those new life goals.

Let's face it, you can't create and launch your own company if you only have an hour a day in which to do it. You can't get fit if you can only squeeze one exercise session into your working week. You can't do all the necessary preparation for that exam if your schedule is already fit to bursting. So in order to move forward you will need to review your day-to-day timetable and be logical with what you can fit in.

I couldn't function without my daily to-do lists: I write several of them a day, and I am learning to be really ruthless about what's important. I really recommend people get into the habit of writing down everything they have to do in their day – from those meetings, the presentations, making those phone calls or answering those emails, as well as all the home chores – write it all down, it makes it so much easier to stay focused. And when you're writing it, be sure to break it into chunks – 'before lunch', 'after lunch', 'evening', or by time, in a calendar. Be specific.

Ask yourself: which of these tasks can I realistically achieve today? How long are they likely to take me? (This is so important when brushing up your time-management skills.) Which of these is really important? What can go to the bottom of the list?

Just writing this down can help you focus, feel more efficient, and just get stuff done. Without a proper list I end up half-doing a lot of my daily tasks, or forgetting something, or never doing any of them really well.

3 TOP TIPS FOR TO-DO LISTS

• Do the Worst Thing First

We all have those dreaded or difficult or most challenging parts of our day, many of which are easily pushed to the bottom of the list. It's much better to just bite the bullet and make a habit of doing one of them each day – ideally while you're fresh and full of energy, first thing in the morning. That way you won't spend the rest of your day dreading it. It's really pleasing to get something horrible off your list!

• Do Five Small Tasks Quickly

Sometimes those tiny jobs get left behind when we're concentrating on the big ones. I often whizz through about five mini-tasks (signing cheques, sending texts, etc.) just to be able to cross something off my list. It gives me the feeling I'm getting somewhere!

• Try the 30-minute Rule

Often we get real blocks about certain tasks in our day – a big filing job, or working out a budget or writing a difficult letter to someone tricky, even doing that horrendous pile of ironing. It really helps to tell yourself you'll just do it for 30 minutes – just so long as you make a start. It's amazing how often that 30 minutes somehow helps break the back of it until the job's done. Often getting started is the worst part.

Bust the Stressors

When I get overwhelmed, I can't do a thing. So throughout the day I try to ask myself, 'What's giving me the biggest stress right now? What can I do about it? Can taking 15 minutes out give me time to reduce the impact that it's having on me? A phone call? A few minutes looking for that vital document I've mislaid? Looking something up on the internet?' I recommend aiming for a stress-busting 15 minutes once or twice a day. It makes such a big difference to your sense of calm!

4 RESEARCH AND PLAN

Your research skills get pretty good when you're an elite athlete. A little knowledge goes a long way. For a start, you need to keep informed about the criteria and targets for selection events, because you don't go to a championship unless you've made the time. Then you need to get to know the track – to be familiar with the climate in the country you may be competing in. How will this affect your performance? How can you tailor your training around that? What time of day will you be competing? How will your body cope with that, and how can you be prepared for it? What about your flight? How many time zones are you crossing? What sort of food will the airline be serving? How will that affect your normal eating habits? Absolutely everything has an impact on your performance when you're competing at elite level. I remember at Athens having to be constantly aware of maintaining my energy levels between heats, semi-finals, and finals. It is really important to refuel after a race. So even though I'd just won the gold medal at the 800 metres, I had to ask Sally Gunnell to give me the nuts and drinks I'd passed to her earlier in the day for when she interviewed me after my rounds and victory lap. That's because I really needed to stay on form for the 1,500 metres. Forget the Champagne! That's how focused I had to be.

And then you have to know your opposition. Who's in your race? How have they been performing during that season? What are their tactics? You learn that people basically don't change their tactics all that much, or their way of running.

For example, in the 800-metre final at Athens, I knew Meredith Rainey was a natural pacemaker and would go off really fast, and that Maria Mutola was a natural tactician and that she would hold back in the final. So my plan was to run as evenly as possible over the whole 800 metres, running even sets of 200m, and conserve my energy for the end. So although it looked as though I was far off the pace – people may have been wondering how on earth was I going to get there – I kept a level head, and in the end I felt great coming down the home straight because I hadn't wasted my energy earlier in the race. And, of course, my plan won me the race ...

You can relate this approach to any goal you're striving for, really. If you're hoping to change careers, or get a new job, or to get fit, preparation is key. How much do you know about that new job market, or healthy eating, or to get fit and in training for that 5k run? Say you want to set up your own business: you need a really firm idea of the market, competitors, finances. Be willing to listen and learn and, most of all, be focused on what you're trying to achieve. Make all the plans, do your research, and increase your knowledge.

Then you can say to yourself, 'I have done the work. I can't be any more prepared. So I have to give it a go.'

5 CREATE 'TEAM YOU'

As an athlete, you rely totally on your top team of coaches, physios, nutrition experts and mentors to help you reach your very best condition physically and mentally. Their expertise, energy, vision and motivation are key if an athlete is to achieve his or her goals. Without my team (Dave Arnold, my first coach, Margo Jennings, my newer coach, my physio Alison Rose, my team support Zara Hyde Peters, Tony Whiteman and Andy Graffin, my training partners, and the doctors who kept me healthy) I could never have won double Olympic gold. And without friends and family – positive people who always believed in me – I could certainly never have kept smiling through the hard times, defeat and dreaded injury.

Even now, even though I consider myself incredibly 'hands on' with all my projects (OK, a bit of a control freak!), I realise that I can't do everything on my own – and that I don't know everything, so if there's an opportunity to delegate some of my responsibilities, I do. And I have gathered good people to help me.

This idea of 'Team You' is a key component of the Backing Talent seminars we run for promising young athletes, one of the initiatives we launched with the Dame Kelly Holmes Legacy Trust and 'On Camp with

Kelly', my mentoring and education initiative which I have been running since 2004.

We ask the young athletes to think about their 'team' – those people who help them within their sport and beyond, those who help keep their life in balance. They're given a worksheet to help them compile this 'Team You', and we suggest that team-mates could include parents/relations, friends, training partners, coaches (their overall coach and specialist coaches), teachers, medical and sports science support – such as physios and GPs, nutritionists/psychologists, and employers if relevant. The other important thing is that these are all positive people around you – not negative.

It's a good exercise for anyone: ask yourself who you need to help you reach that dream goal, or be more successful in your life. How would you go about creating your 'Team You'? It doesn't have to be as formal as the teams we ask our young athletes to create. These can just be people you might need to help you move forward – and you can tell them as little or as much as you wish about your goal.

So have a think: who is your support – partner, friend, family member, colleague? Who do you know who can help you achieve your goal? Who has the expertise to talk to you about how to go about doing what it is you want to do? Do you need to see a careers advisor? Perhaps you need help with childcare/pet-sitting to free you up in the evenings? Or a cleaner who can just help take the pressure off? How is your work/life balance? Are you too overwrought at work to put any new dreams into action? In that case, is it time to think about delegating some of your workload? And who do you know who can inspire you, or encourage you, or just help you troubleshoot when you need support?

Think about the people around you who can help make your life easier. Here are some questions we ask our young athletes to think about when creating their own team. Sit down and work through them with your 'team' in mind:

- Is each 'team member' aware of your goals and dreams?

- Do they know how you are trying to reach those goals?

- Do they know how they are helping you?

- Are they doing everything they can to help you?

6 GIVE YOURSELF A 'HEAD EMPTY'

I always know when I'm getting stressed. It starts creeping up on me – I become aware there's so much going on in my head – where I should be, what I should be doing and what I haven't done yet, and what's going to happen if I don't do it soon – and it all becomes a massive, urgent blur. Nothing is getting done. I'm losing control! It happens to me frequently, and when it does I know I need a 'head empty'.

So wherever I am I stop, get some paper and write down everything that's on my mind – what I haven't done, what I have to do – and then I work out the top priorities. I list them in order of urgency, but I try to focus on prioritising two or three items – just enough to relieve that feeling of stress or panic.

Sometimes just 5 minutes of 'time out' will do the trick – so afterwards I stick the telly on (reality telly does it for me!) or, ideally, get outside.

I'm lucky to live in the country so I only have to open the door to see something green which has an immediately calming effect on me. People underestimate how powerful the countryside can be. But even if you live in a big built-up city, just getting outdoors to the nearest park or lake or garden, or standing in front of a lovely big leafy tree can rebalance your brain, and switch off that stress button. A five-minute 'head empty' is the best way to get perspective – so remember, write it down, get outside, look at something green! Then get back to it.

Clear Your Head: Get Outdoors

There's a huge body of research to show that getting out in the garden or walking in the countryside can lower stress levels and boost mental health. One study, published in the *Journal of Environmental Psychology*, found that people exposed to greenery had lower blood pressure and an elevated mood within minutes, compared to those who sat in a windowless room. And a study in the *American Journal of Preventive Medicine* found that surrounding yourself with greenery can help you stay healthy and less stressed. Other studies have shown that surgery patients with views over greenery recover faster than those without them. Experts say that creating a connection with the natural world is good for you mentally as well as physically.

WHAT TO DO TODAY FOR SUCCESS TOMORROW

✓ *Assess how organised you are* – right now. Which areas do you need to improve on in order to feel more in control of your life?

✓ *Get yourself a diary* – think of it as your companion on your journey.

✓ *Start researching and planning what you need to do to action your goal.* Twenty minutes a day is a good place to start.

✓ *Sit down and think about who would be in 'Team You'.* Who can help you move forward in your new life direction?

CHAPTER 3

Thinking Positive: Secrets to Staying Confident

'*If you want to succeed at anything you have to believe in yourself.*'

— Kelly

People often ask me what goes through an athlete's mind when they're in a race. The truth is, it really varies. Sometimes you're so focused you know you're going to run really well. You feel good, confident and, in a way, excited. Other times you line up feeling nervous: you have these niggling thoughts in your head that the other athletes are faster, stronger or better. Or you may be doing well until a small doubt creeps into your mind – and if you don't get your concentration back, you've lost the race. Nerves can also get the better of you. If you are aware of who is in front of you all the time, people pushing and tripping, then you're probably not going to do that well and are losing far too much energy.

Then there are the times when you're in 'the zone' – as I was in the 2004 Olympics. Call it tunnel vision or call it total self-belief. Whatever it was, I was in my own zone: I knew where I was going, when I was going to go, what I needed to do, and that was it. I don't think anyone could have touched me ...

BELIEVING IN YOURSELF

By now, hopefully you're thinking that you could make some positive changes in your life.

The next important step is a big one. You need to *believe in yourself*.

It's such a simple phrase, isn't it? But for many people, self-belief is the sticking point – the hugest challenge of all – especially if they've never been a positive thinker, or they've tried and failed at achieving certain goals in the past, and as a result have lost self-confidence.

I believe that, to a certain extent, people are either optimists or pessimists by nature. Some people are simply born with self-belief and the ability to think positively and to be optimistic about life and the future. Others aren't. Some people see barriers well before they actually face them, or doubt a good outcome every time. It's like that saying – is your glass half-full or half-empty? (Mine is always half-full!)

I strongly feel that everyone can be helped to feel more confident and motivated, with the right attitude and the right people behind them.

I'm a positive thinker by nature – you can't be an Olympic champion without believing in yourself. That's not boasting, that's a fact: an athlete at my level doesn't go out there thinking, 'I can't do this' or 'I can't do that.' If you really believe that you can achieve, if you have enough evidence for it, and if it's been ingrained in you over and over that you *can*, you'll at least do everything possible to perfect the skills of your sport and to improve your performance in order to come out on top. And you'll believe you can. That's what makes a champion, as opposed to someone who's very good at their sport.

Don't get me wrong: there have been times in my life that my self-belief, my ability to think positive about my own capabilities, have taken a massive tumble and I have lost a lot of confidence about my dream becoming a reality – big time! (I'll talk more about that in the next chapter.)

However, as an elite athlete you're taught a variety of really powerful techniques to help master positive thinking – techniques that can be applied not only to racing, but to other goals – losing weight, switching careers, learning another skill, making various changes in your life.

When people say 'I can't', I want to say to them, 'There's no such thing as "can't".' That doesn't mean things are not hard. But 'I *can't*'? I don't agree with that.

As long as your goal is realistic (and saying 'I want to wake up tomorrow on a luxury yacht in the Bahamas' isn't – well, for most people!), and as long as it's within your capabilities (as we discussed in Chapter 1), then there really is no such thing as 'can't'.

People often say 'I can't' because they're scared of failure, or are worried about letting other people down. Think about that next time you say to yourself, 'I can't.' Try to get to the bottom of your self-doubt. Why are you really saying 'I can't'? Does it just seem too hard? Or perhaps it might not come to you as quickly as you'd like? Remember, if you want something enough and are prepared to give 100 per cent to achieving it, then you can. You just have to believe you can, and keep reminding yourself that you can, and be patient.

So for all those people who simply weren't born positive thinkers – and for those, like me, who are positive thinkers who need a refresher course from time to time, let's look at some of the tools I've learned and which have helped me in my athletics career and beyond.

YOUR GLORY LIST

What Am I Good At?

In Chapter 1 we talked about ways of refining your hopes and dreams into specifics. One of the key exercises was to write down your talents and abilities (see page 9). That's a good exercise to look at again now, but this time, think even more broadly.

What have you done in your life that you're proud of? What kind of compliments do people give you? What are your personality strengths?

I did a similar exercise back in 2003 and it told me a lot about myself.

I had just started training with a new coach, an American called Margo Jennings. Margo had been coaching Mozambique athlete Maria Mutola for years, but she agreed to train me alongside Maria while the two of us were both staying and training in South Africa.

Margo's an incredible woman, a former schoolteacher and a fantastic coach – really inspiring. I had been struck by her motivational approach – you could see how it had shaped Maria Mutola: Maria always had an air of confidence. She was strong, positive, a champion with no self-doubts. Back then Maria definitely had more confidence than me; at that stage I'd been beset by injury and setbacks. Margo's motivating approach was just what I needed to help boost my self-belief, which is why I'd asked her to take me on.

The first exercise that Margo asked me to do was to write down a list of my strengths, and then my weaknesses.

My list of personality strengths was pretty long – two pages' worth in fact! Here are some of the highlights:

'Drive, determination, guts, ability to withstand pain, disciplined, experienced, intelligence, courageous, fearless, "eye-of-the-tiger" mentality, ability to focus and concentrate, desire, hunger, commitment, trust, honesty, strong, good speed, excellent form, motivated, goal-orientated, faith in coach's programme, willingness to learn, open-minded, flexible, good traveller, good friend ...'

These were based on who I thought I was because of my past successes and my perceived talents. I had won eight international medals so I must have done something right.

As for the weaknesses – I could only list two:

'Injuries; lack of confidence due to the injuries'.

It's a brilliant exercise to do. Try it now – but just focus on your strengths for now – leave the list of weaknesses till later. Give yourself half an hour – or dip in and out of it during the day as things occur to you.

So get a piece of paper, or open your diary and really think about all your past successes, or gifts, or talents. Go back to childhood, working through the years to the present day – making a list of everything you have achieved throughout your life. Perhaps you were captain of the school netball team, or awarded a prize for a great piece of work? You may have sailed through exams, or won a cross-country race at school or made it through a tough interview, bagging that job against the odds. Or perhaps you were praised for some impressive achievement.

- How has this shaped your personality?
- Are you brave, hard-working, kind, patient?

However insignificant it may seem, write it down.

This is your 'glory list' – this is *evidence* of what you can do. It has real value because it reinforces your strengths, past achievements – and reminds you that you *can* succeed. Everyone has a talent – you have abilities that someone else hasn't. So here's where you sing your own praises.

It's amazing how quickly this kind of exercise gets you thinking more positively. I think it gets you believing you are capable of doing things and also gives you a pat on the back!

And it somehow gives you a glimmer of hope. A lot of people will do this exercise and think, 'Yes, I had forgotten I had achieved that.' And this leads on to, 'So maybe I can do something significant again after all.'

Doing this exercise for Margo back in 2003 really helped us move forward as a team. Margo's approach went like this: if I could only put two weaknesses on my list, and one of them was caused by the other, then solving the problems would be fairly straightforward. My lack of confidence was based on the fact that I kept getting injured. It wasn't lack of belief in my ability to achieve, or to be even better than I was.

So in order to move forward, we had to re-evaluate everything that had happened to me so far, to try and get some of my injury problems solved. On top of that, Margo aimed to build up my self-confidence by reminding me what I had achieved during my training, giving me new targets, and by generally inspiring me.

So let's tackle your weaknesses – it's time to write that second list. Don't dwell too much on this list – you're not aiming for quantity here! Instead, just focus on the weaknesses that you feel may be stopping you from moving forward in life. Write them in a list next to your strengths.

Now try looking at your strengths alongside your weaknesses. Try to see if any of your strengths cancel out your weaknesses. You're aiming to strike a balance here, at least. So if, for example, you list 'lack of organisation' in your weaknesses list, but have identified 'good delegator' in your positives, you can see how you may have already overcome this weakness! Or at least you may now be able to find ways to counter it.

Really try to challenge all your supposed 'weaknesses' – are you really being fair to yourself? Look back over your past and try hard to find evidence to the contrary. Hopefully you'll be left with a much smaller list of weaknesses that you need to work on, which won't seem nearly as overwhelming.

Finally, aim to work through your 'weaknesses' list one by one. Try to devise ways in which you can tackle them one step at a time. What can you do to become more organised, for example? You're aiming for realistic solutions, or at least to start thinking about how to create different routes to reach your desired goal.

Review your progress ... It's a good idea, too, to look back at the action plan list you made in Chapters 1 and 2. See what you have achieved this far. How many of those tiny stepping stones have you crossed? What have you crossed off your list? Above all, how are you feeling about edging closer to your goal? All the work you've done so far is really important, and now's the time to take stock and acknowledge how far you've already come in your new direction.

'*Reading this book is a start, but it's down to you to make things happen.*'

– *Kelly*

TALKING POSITIVE: THE POWER OF MANTRAS

There's real power in what they call 'self-talk' or affirmations – repeating positive words or sayings to yourself to build on your confidence levels. When Margo Jennings used to fax me my weekly training programmes, they were always headed with an inspiring motivational mantra. It was her way of helping get me into 'the zone'. For example, I would have to focus on these:

'I am strong, not tired.'

'I am fast, not sluggish.'

'I am an aggressive warrior, not an anxious wimp.'

If you tell yourself something often enough, you start to believe it! There is a theory that if you repeat an action 21 times you will make positive changes. So, for example, if you stop eating sweets for 21 days, you are more likely to keep that up and less likely to crave them any more. When I was at Athens I had a lot of motivational sayings on the wall – and good luck messages from people saying they really believed in me. It made me think, 'Yes, I'm ready, I can do this ... '

'Life's challenges are not supposed to paralyse you; they're supposed to help you discover who you are. Now you have to go for it.'

– Kelly

So, write down your goal on a piece of paper, cut it out and stick it on the wall where you can't fail to see it. (Keep moving it about, or write it on a different coloured paper every few days so you don't stop noticing it!)

Next, put motivational words in visible places to remind yourself every day of what you can do – and what you intend to do. Anything that you hear or read – either specifically about your goal or just about success in general and which you find inspiring – will do. Copy them out, then stick them on your walls, desk, computer, bathroom mirror or the fridge as a constant reminder that you, too, can achieve what you want.

FIND YOURSELF A POSITIVE THINKING MANTRA

Try mine out for size:

- **'Anything is possible; you just have to believe it.'**

- **'Live your dreams; don't let your dreams outlive you.'**

- **'Always give 100 per cent so you can at least say you tried – so much better than living with regrets.'**

Try these inspirational quotes from famous people:

'The world makes way for the man who knows where he is going' – *Ralph Waldo Emerson*

'Goals are dreams with deadlines' – *Diana Scharf Hunt*

'First say to yourself what you would be: and then do what you have to do' – *Epictetus*

'Success is liking yourself, liking what you do, and liking how you do it' – *Maya Angelou*

'You are never too old to set another goal or to dream a new dream' – *C S Lewis*

EYE-TO-EYE CONTACT

This is another technique I'd use. I used to stare at myself in the mirror before a really big championship. I'd look myself bang in the eye, breathe deeply, and repeat to myself, 'Come on, Kelly, this is it. You can do it.' Again, it was about getting positive and focused – getting in the zone. You might feel a bit daft doing it, but it helps, particularly just before a specific stressful challenge such as a job interview or exam or race. Just maybe avoid doing it in front of other people!

Besides, when you're pushing your body to the limits, as I often had to do, both as a PTI and an athlete, self-talk like this is absolutely crucial: you just don't get through the challenges unless you believe in yourself.

For example, one of the toughest physical challenges of my life took place when I was a PTI in the Women's Royal Army Corps in 1993/4. As part of the amalgamation of the WRAC and the Army, I had to complete a really gruelling pre-selection course which you had to pass if you were to be accepted onto the Physical Training Corps training course. We were in direct competition with the men, and we had to excel in all the physical tests, just as they did, in order to be considered.

There were 30 of us on the course – including five women. The physical fitness tests were really tough and included heaves (straight-arm chin-ups), an assault course, fitness test runs, gymnastics, and command task skills.

Very worst of all was the log run: this involved running with a massive log, six to eight to a team, for 3 miles – each of us placed at intervals along the log. It was even harder given that we were all different heights – the weight of that log on your back and arms was unbearable.

The instructors were screaming at us as we sprinted from Aldershot to some sand dunes – which we then had to climb! I can honestly say that running up and down those sand dunes – which give way under your feet – while carrying the dead weight of a log was horrendous. And then, once we had finished, we had to drop the log, swap our boots for trainers and run back to camp!

Despite the exhaustion, I was so determined to get a place on the course that I ran as hard as I could, and ended up beating everyone back. Every muscle in my body was screaming in pain. But for me the only way to get through it was to keep totally focused, completely positive – to keep on and on silently repeating to myself, 'Come on, you can do it. I can do it. I am not going to be beaten.' The message must have reached my aching legs and arms! They didn't give up on me. And it paid off – I was one of only five people from the group to be accepted onto the course – and the only woman!

Chances are you're not going to be carrying a massive log for 3 miles up and down sand dunes, but the same principle applies. You have to tell yourself you can achieve your goal – and keep repeating that to yourself – on paper, in the mirror or just in your head, until your brain learns how to make it happen!

You'll only be able to convince yourself, though, if you are confident you have done all the preparation – whether that's doing all your research for a job interview, doing all the necessary studying for your adult education course, or committing to enough exercise classes or a training programme so faithfully that you know you're going to be in shape to manage your first 10k race.

Knowing that I'd done all the planning, preparation and training when I went out on the track certainly helped me. It may not have always given me the outcome I wanted, every time, especially coming back from injury, but you have to go out there – on the track, or in the workplace, wherever – believing in yourself. Otherwise you will not do a thing. And knowing that you're *prepared* is a huge part of that battle.

WHAT'S YOUR GOAL?
MY GOLDEN RULES OF WEIGHT LOSS

- **Rethink your fats: cut back on saturated fats (found in cakes, biscuits, pies and fatty meats) and instead try to get more good fats into your daily diet (good sources include oily fish, nuts, seeds, avocados, olive oil).**

- **Don't starve: eat three meals a day and eat healthy snacks regularly – ideally eat something nutritious every three hours. This helps keep your blood sugar levels stable, prevents cravings and fills you up. Starving yourself slows down your metabolism, which is not what you want when you're trying to shift the weight.**

- **Swap refined carbohydrates (cakes, biscuits, white bread, white rice, pasta) – for wholegrain varieties. They provide more nutrients and help fill you up for longer.**

- **Get enough good protein: aim to incorporate lean proteins (such as fish, cheese and dairy products, lean meat, chicken, nuts) into each meal – and each snack. Protein helps keep you feeling satisfied for longer.**

- **Rethink your portion sizes: swap three big meals for five to six smaller ones.**

DO YOUR HOMEWORK

Now's the time to go back and look at the preparation work you started in Chapter 2. What did you establish you needed to do to prepare for your goal? If your aim is to start your own business, how is your research going? Are you familiar with the market – the competition? How well do you know the product or service you'll be selling? Your knowledge has to be watertight if you're to succeed in a new arena. Have you got the right support, and have you spoken to experts in the field?

If your goal is to lose weight, perhaps you've tried and failed in the past. Have you revisited your efforts to find out why you may have failed? Is there a particular area that you find difficult? Were you too strict with yourself? Perhaps you didn't seek the right support – would a weight loss group be a good idea to help keep you motivated? Or maybe you lacked inspiration when it came to healthy eating? Perhaps you could invest in some good low-fat cookbooks, or team up with a buddy for support and ideas? It could be that you need to focus on exercise alongside your healthier eating habits; it's the only way to really improve your physical and fitness levels. Remember, your head can either stop you – or make you achieve anything you want.

It will really help you to keep going back over your stepping stones or that 'success flowchart' from

Chapter 1, where you listed all the elements and stages that are crucial to attaining your goal.

I can't emphasise enough how important it is to do all your background work – you just can't reach the level of self-belief you need unless you feel prepared.

> '*Turn your negative thoughts about making changes into positive ones.*'
>
> – Kelly

VISUALISE YOUR SUCCESS

Can you really visualise yourself achieving your goal? Can you see yourself in your brand new job, at your new desk, confident and capable? Have you envisaged enjoying your new slim, toned body, or crossing the line of that 5k run elated and feeling great about yourself? It may be a cliché, but seeing is believing – even if it's in your imagination.

Sports psychology is an increasingly important part of an elite athlete's training. It involves using a set of techniques or mindsets to help athletes work through specific problems that may be affecting their confidence and performance.

Sports psychologists are consulted to help beat overwhelming pre-race nerves, or to help troubleshoot a problem – such as getting back into a positive frame of mind following injury. There are times when an athlete's head tells him he can't push himself harder in training, or perhaps he is getting overly anxious about his rivals, and it leads to doubts about his performance on the track. That's when some useful sports psychology approaches can work wonders.

Take visualisation. It's a technique we pass on to the young athletes I mentor – in order to help keep their frame of mind positive.

The idea is you create a detailed picture in your head of yourself achieving a certain goal, or improving your performance, dealing with pressure or overcoming your nerves. You focus really hard – creating an image in your mind – and see yourself going through all the stages until you reach that goal.

I used to do this all the time. You may see yourself running the tactics you had wanted to run, but hadn't been able to. Or, if you are experiencing really bad pre-race nerves, you see yourself walking on to the track feeling calm, focused and positive. Athletes who have been struggling with meeting their training targets may be encouraged to visualise themselves feeling strong, full of energy and vitality so that they can move on to the next stage of training.

I suppose visualisation is about training the brain – being clear about what you want, and letting your brain find a way of making it happen for you. And this can work equally well with losing weight, getting fitter, succeeding at that job interview or achieving any goal you set yourself, really. In fact, psychologists say that the brain doesn't distinguish between a really vividly imagined event and a real one, so the more you visualise, the more your brain and body are ready to make it happen.

Athletes do a lot of mental rehearsal – they create the experience of winning, they live out that success in their heads. The key is to regularly visualise your goal – doing this again and again means the image becomes incredibly clear to your mind – you can see what success looks like, how it feels – the visualisation has to be as real, detailed, clear and vivid as possible.

TRY THIS!

Sit or lie down and get comfortable. Close your eyes and breathe deeply and slowly – in for a count of 4, out for a count of 4. Repeat this until you feel the tension gradually leave your body. When you're feeling calm and relaxed, start to imagine yourself achieving something positive that will take you forward to your goal.

Take your time – slowly build the image and make it real. You're after a full picture of your desired goal. See it, notice the details, the sounds, the sights – really live it. You're practising for reality by visualising – and making a successful outcome more likely. Plus when you get into this state of complete focus and visualisation, it really helps with your planning. You're fully prepared because you've rehearsed and anticipated all the necessary steps.

The key is to repeat this visualisation as often as you possibly can – first thing in the morning as you're lying in bed, or last thing at night, or whenever you get a chance during the day.

STAYING CALM: RELAXATION

If being calm, in control and fully prepared is what you need to succeed, then panic and anxiety are the enemy. As an athlete, there are occasions when nerves take over and you just can't summon the mental energy and self-belief to get you through. It all goes pear-shaped!

It happened to me in the Gothenburg World Championships in 1995.

I had been having a great year – I'd won every race I'd entered, including the European Cup, all the grand prix, the Inter-Services Championships and the AAA

Championships in Birmingham – and even achieved a personal best for the 800 metres of 1:57.56. So I approached the World Championships with great confidence, determined to go for gold in the 800m and the 1,500m.

But on the day of the 1,500m final, a strange thing happened to me: from the moment I woke up, all I could do was think about the race – I just couldn't get it out of my head. As an athlete you try not to think *too* much about an imminent race – it can drain you of nervous energy. (You should have done all the visualisation and race tactics the night before.)

But from waking up at 7 a.m. until the race – which was starting at 5:25 p.m. – all I could think about was, 'Only 10 hours to go and it will be over. Only 8 hours and it will be over. Just 6 more hours and it will all be over,' on and on in my head like that all day.

My main opponent was the Algerian champion Hassiba Boulmerka – and I kept envisaging the two of us neck and neck in a huge struggle to the finish line. It was really stressful. Even when I had a rest that afternoon I couldn't get the image of the track out of my mind. Even while I was trying to switch off by reading a magazine I could see myself running around the track – with me struggling down the home straight. I just couldn't relax. And when the time finally came, and we were at the track about to line up for the start of the race, I remember looking at the clock in the stadium thinking, 'Four minutes and it will be over ...'

It was a tough race with a lot of bunching and tripping and changing pace. I was aware of it all! Three laps, 2 laps, 1 lap on the lap counter. As we went round the last bend, Boulmerka made her break. I left it a fraction too late to attack, and couldn't quite catch her. She stormed home the winner, and I was gutted. It was a race I knew I could have won. I won a silver, but I was in the best shape of my life and I had messed everything up by worrying about the race all day. I was so exhausted even before the race, I blew it. I was gutted.

That race taught me an all-important lesson about controlling my nerves, and adrenaline – and it's a lesson for everyone really: RELAX!

As an athlete you need adrenaline to get fired up for a race. But if you have too much of it – you've lost it. Back then I hadn't learned to control my nerves, as I did later in my career. You learn to distract yourself from the race and opposition beforehand by switching off, relaxing and chatting to people, flicking through magazines, listening to music, controlling your breathing. You're relaxing, but you're positive and you're calm in the belief that you will be able to do it when the time comes and you get on that track. It's like putting a pair of blinkers on so you can't see the people you perceive as threats, and you can't see anything that may distract you – in a negative way – from your goal.

Learning to control your breathing helps massively. When you are breathing deeply (in through your nose, feeling your lungs inflating with air as you push your abdomen out, holding it in for a count of two and then breathing out hard and fast while drawing in your abdomen), then your muscles relax, your heart-rate follows and your mind calms down, too. You're in the best position then to think rationally about the challenge ahead, and to work through any fears or worries calmly.

So when athletes become overly anxious about their rivals, we train them to shift this thought pattern by slowing down their breathing, and then switch their focus so that they are able to think rationally. Rather than thinking that everyone else in the race is in much better shape, the athlete learns to consider the possibility that the other athletes might have also been injured and that this is their first race out, or that they might not be feeling well, or that they've missed a month of training for some reason. Or, believe it or not, that they may be even more nervous.

You won't know how others are going to perform until you're up against them, so you can only be in control of your own life, your own performance.

It's the same with a job interview, exam or any situation where you're coming up against potential rivals. Learning to relax and silence that voice of panic inside your head – countering every negative thought with a calm, positive response – means you're better able to focus on what you *can* achieve.

Everyone who takes on a challenge will have an element of doubt – that it will all go wrong or will be just too tough to overcome. 'I won't be able to lose weight – I never have in the past.' Or, 'I'm just not going to be able to pass my exams – I've skipped too much revision.' Or, 'I'll lose it in that interview – I always do.' This is normal panic and apprehension about the outcome. And this is when the deep breathing exercises, the mind-calming strategies, really work. It is also where that positive self-belief needs to kick back in.

When you're feeling calm and relaxed, it's the ideal opportunity to programme your mind more effectively! So now is a good time to focus on your own hard work – go back over everything you have done so far to achieve your goal – like a mental checklist, and remind yourself you're capable of moving forward with it.

Repeat one of these mantras to yourself: 'I can do it,' 'I am confident and focused,' 'I'm an achiever' – or whatever works for you ...

TRY THIS!

The key is to breathe from the diaphragm, rather than from your upper chest. We tend to breathe from our upper chest in times of anxiety – it's part of the body's fight-or-flight response. But when you breathe deeply from the abdomen, you get into a real state of calm: your body relaxes and your mind follows.

Lie down and put one hand on your stomach and one on your upper chest.

Now take a deep breath, and see which hand moves.

Breathe in to a count of four, feeling your belly rise up under your hand. Then focus on releasing your breath for a count of four as you draw your abdomen right in. Repeat four or five times.

Do this two or three times a day – sitting, standing or lying down.

THE 'WHY NOT?' APPROACH

Here's a great exercise to do when you're feeling you've set your sights too high, or are losing motivation. Play at being your own devil's advocate, and then your own coach.

First, give yourself lots of reasons why you shouldn't/can't achieve your goal – and then see what counter-arguments you can come up with.

Start by listing every reason you have for *not* going on with your goal. For example – if your goal is to start a new career but you've somehow lost momentum, start by listing all those reasons you're giving yourself NOT to go on:

- It's too difficult at this stage of my life.

- I'm not qualified enough.

- I haven't got the time.

- Do I really want a new stress in my life?

Now, be your own coach, with a counter-argument for each barrier you've come up with:

- **It's too difficult at this stage of my life:** *Rubbish, people are changing career direction all the time these days, regardless of their age. Besides, my experience will count for something.*

- **I'm not qualified enough:** *But I've looked into that extra qualification I might need, and I could actually manage it if I did that distance-learning course.*

- **I haven't got the time:** *I could manage it if I got some help with childcare and swapped my evening commitments around.*

- **Do I really want a new stress in my life?:** *It's not stress, it's a challenge and it's good for the brain and my energy to stretch myself.*

You see how it works. Whether you're losing motivation to shed some pounds, start running or move to another part of the world, having this kind of dialogue with yourself is a really great way to be your own motivating coach, and also to explore some of the challenges that your new goal might be raising.

SURROUND YOURSELF WITH POSITIVE PEOPLE

In Chapter 2 we talked about enlisting 'Team You' – that is, creating a list of people who can help you move forwards with your goal. This could take the form of a 'panel of experts' such as a careers advisor, business mentor, a good friend who can tell you how great you are, and a good babysitter or dog-walker who can physically free you up to spend time on your goal.

Make sure that among your team you have at least one 'goal buddy'. By that I mean a really positive person who is aware of the goal you have set for yourself and is happy to be there for you along the way – if you want to talk through ideas or offload when it all gets tough.

Even if you don't consult that person or people all the time (they might find that a bit much!), remember it has to be someone – or even a few people – who can say a few inspiring words or just believe in you, or give you that bit of hope or motivation when you're slipping out of your positive mindset.

Everyone has a downtime when they're chasing a goal. It doesn't matter how motivated, how determined, how stubborn or driven you are, there will always be something that knocks you.

In my career I certainly needed a motivating influence – somebody I could confide in and say, 'I've struggled here.' For me, Margo Jennings was the great motivator – she was great at keeping me believing in myself. My mum was great, too! She always believed in me, always spurred me on and kept on reminding me I could do it.

And although I'm not a professional athlete any more, I still need that kind of encouragement! We all have to find someone to accept that role in life. So it's time to bring on board that important person who will be part of your dream, to stay beside you no matter what, and ride the journey with you.

FIVE-MINUTE MOTIVATOR: THE NAME GAME

Here's a great exercise I used to do when I needed to remind myself I could do it.

Take the letters of your name and write a positive word for each letter – a positive word that gives you a lift, describes you now or embodies the qualities you have that will help you achieve your goal:

K – knowledgeable
E – energetic
L – living
L – life
Y – yes, I can do it

H – hard working
O – opportunities
L – learn (never stop)
M – motivated
E – excellence
S – success

Your turn!

Positive Thinking Made Easy

Focusing on good, positive things as they happen can make you happier, and also be a great motivator. In a study published in the journal *Emotion*, college students were first asked to rate how happy they were with their lives. They were then asked to keep a daily diary of their positive and negative feelings as they happened. At the end of the study the students were asked again to rate how happy they were with their lives. The study showed that those who experienced little moments of happiness throughout their day – just appreciating small good things as they happened – were overall the happiest and most contented people.

WHAT TO DO TODAY FOR SUCCESS TOMORROW

✓ *Write your 'glory list'* – include every
achievement, compliment and success in your
past – however small. It will remind you that
you are capable of further success.

✓ *Find yourself a mantra* – positive, affirming
statements that train your brain to think more
positively.

✓ *Try creative visualisation:* imagine yourself
achieving your goal – note every detail so it
becomes as realistic as possible. Spend at
least 10 minutes a day – more if possible –
building and reinforcing this image.

✓ *Learn to relax:* practise deep 'abdominal'
breathing at least once every day.

✓ *Be your own coach:* for every reason why you
shouldn't pursue your goal, give yourself a
really good reason for sticking with it! The
more reasons, the better.

CHAPTER 4

Overcoming Obstacles: The Will to Win

'To succeed in any walk of life you must have passion, desire and the will to overcome any obstacle in your path ...'

– from my book,
Black, White and Gold

One thing you can guarantee when you're daring to follow a dream is that it's not going to be plain sailing. Not all of the time, anyway. And sometimes that can come as a big shock, particularly if you believe you've been doing everything right, and giving it your all, every step of the way.

When I say 'doing everything right', I mean you have considered every detail, or have been following those key stepping stones we've been looking at throughout this book – goal-setting, planning, switching on a positive mindset, and so on.

But the truth is, however realistic and sensible you are about goal-setting, however carefully you do all the preparation and planning, chances are you are going encounter some major obstacles or massive pitfalls along the way. And even if you've followed all the advice in Chapter 3 about how to really believe in yourself and *see* yourself succeeding, these obstacles can still knock you for six and potentially make you want to give up. It has happened to me many times, both in my Army life and athletics career.

That's why this chapter – on overcoming obstacles – is such a crucial one.

Over the years there have certainly been times when it seemed that everything was against me – I felt cursed – certain people, illness, injury (lots of that!) and negative circumstances generally. And if I hadn't picked myself up each time, gradually learning how to bounce back from disappointments and overcome the huge barriers that seemed to stand in my way, I'd never have got my dream job – being a PTI in the Army – nor would I have had such success in athletics. And I'd never have won two gold medals in the Olympics – that's for sure.

So what kind of obstacles are you likely to meet? I can only go from my own experiences, so I've listed them under five key sections in this chapter. I suspect these are the kind of hurdles that most people will encounter when they've decided to make a big change and follow a dream.

They are:

1. difficult people (and difficult, awkward conversations)
2. unexpected setbacks

3. awkward (or tough) decisions

4. having to change your plans at the last minute and when things go wrong

5. hitting rock bottom – complete emotional fallout.

I'm not claiming to have a magic formula to make these obstacles disappear – and I'm no psychologist. But over the years I've learned valuable lessons and picked up some useful skills that somehow got me *experience* through mine. Hopefully they will help you, too.

OBSTACLE 1: DEALING WITH DIFFICULT PEOPLE AND TRICKY CONVERSATIONS

Rule number one: Always remember, no one person holds your destiny.

The ideal scenario for setting yourself a new goal or new life direction is that you will be surrounded by positive, encouraging people who want you to succeed and who will do all they can to make that happen. Like the kind of employer who *listens* when you say you'd like to try working in a different department or going for a promotion, and who helps put things in motion.

Or an instructor at your gym who agrees to help you train for that first 5k race, and keeps encouraging you along the way. Or a friend or relative who knows how many times you've tried (and failed) to lose weight, who knows how bad it is making you feel, and who this time pledges to help you do it and stands by you throughout.

Sadly, however, we occasionally meet people who don't want us to succeed, for whatever reason (which often we can never work out). You know the type – people who obstruct you, or make things difficult, or just don't give you a chance. It could be an employer who isn't prepared to help you move upwards and doesn't give you credit for your role within the company, or someone who could have a really positive influence with a new business plan or idea, but just doesn't bother. Someone close to you who doesn't really want you to lose weight or get fit in case you 'change' and become more confident. Or a person who doesn't give you or your ambitions any credibility, who perhaps brushes away your ideas dismissively, or even laughs at you.

It's tough when you meet people like this (even tougher if they're close to you). It's frustrating when you come across people in power who just aren't approachable or helpful, or look down on you or don't give you any respect. Personally I think when certain people move on to higher things in life, they get on a power trip and forget what it's like to be at the bottom desperately wanting to work your way up.

Sometimes it just comes down to a personality clash: you just can't seem to get on an even keel with someone, and it feels as though you're just not being given the chance you want. The root of the problem could be jealousy, or there may be a whole lot of other unfathomable reasons. But it's very challenging if you're on the receiving end.

I remember one horrible situation with an Army officer – it certainly falls into the 'personality clash' category. As I've said earlier, from the age of 14 I had dreamed of becoming a PTI (physical training instructor), and once I'd been accepted into the Army and was working as a driver, I did all I could to move sideways from that role to becoming a PTI. Believe me, I pulled out all the stops to do this – volunteering at lunchtimes to go to the gym with the PTI guys, and getting really involved in physical training sessions.

Eventually my commitment paid off, and I was admitted onto a pre-selection course at the Duchess of Kent Barracks in Aldershot. Frustratingly, that didn't work out first time – my co-ordination and skills let me down (certain of my skills such as hockey, badminton, gymnastics and swimming just weren't good enough), and I failed. But I could understand why, and knew what I needed to do to improve.

More determined than ever, I devoted my spare time and all my efforts to training and really perfecting those sports, including going on courses to learn the skills I needed. At the time I was in the Army Athletics team, too, so my fitness levels were really good. It took weeks of focus and determination to get it right next time. The good news was that it worked – I was accepted onto another pre-selection course (this was in 1990). It was a really tough course, and again I gave it my all.

Finally I was selected to go on a nine-month Physical Training course at PT school in Aldershot. My dream had come true (or so I thought). It was tough but physically I had proven myself to be one of the strongest women on the course (and definitely the fastest!).

One of the stages of the course (Leadership and Drill) took place at the Duchess of Kent Barracks. At the time, many of us on the course didn't get on very well with one of the 2nd Lieutenant officers. Early on we got the impression that she seemed to be against us. Whatever we did, we were told we were not up to scratch. In fact, on one occasion during the course, five of us were taken aside and told to 'buck up our ideas'. We couldn't understand why or where this had come from, because we were doing everything we were told to do.

Later on I was one of three in our team to be given a warning. I was shocked and completely baffled – everyone agreed I was completing all the sections well, and was easily as good as the other candidates.

You can imagine how completely gutted I was at the end of the course when I was called into see two of the commanding officers – including that particular officer – to hear that I had failed.

It was completely devastating – particularly as the rest of the platoon was so excited to be passing out. It just made no sense whatsoever. As I heard those words, it was as if she was singlehandedly destroying my future, and shattering my dreams. I couldn't believe it. My world had caved in.

And I dared to tell the commanding officer just that. In fact, I talked back to her (something you just don't do to an officer in the Army!). I was fuming, and felt totally destroyed. I said, 'That's it, I am leaving the Army then.' Just as I was about to walk out the door she had the cheek to say, 'Oh, but we still want you in the cross-country team.' But I'd had enough. I signed the papers, walked out and went home.

About a week later I was asked to go back to the barracks and was given the opportunity to talk it through with the Lieutenant Colonel. At last I was able to tell my side of events. She was clearly furious about what had happened, as she believed I had great potential and would have made an excellent PTI.

So they gave me the opportunity to get back on the course to show what I could do. It was amazing being given a second chance, and I gave it my all again – getting a top-class report, being formally readmitted on the course, and passing it with flying colours.

The bottom line was I knew I hadn't done anything wrong on that course. I gave 100 per cent, as I always do. In time, the truth filtered out. And even though it was a tough, tough time, I got through it and moved on. I was not going to let one sole person ruin my life.

Not everyone is going to face something as potentially dramatic as this scenario. There may be more subtle ways that people are blocking your path. But it really helps to have some strategies up your sleeve so that those difficult people don't wear you down or dent your ambition.

I did learn a lot about myself as a result of this episode, at any rate. It takes a lot to rattle my cage, but when it happens, I react! Big time! Over the years I have learned how to handle difficult situations, and I'm better now at controlling my reactions and emotions. It's hard to do (and I have had to bite my tongue many times), but it's also helpful!

Get Clarity

This is absolutely vital. Everyone needs to take time out to really work out what is going on. Yes, you may well have an immediate emotional response to a situation or an encounter with someone, and let's face it we can't always hold our tongue when we feel someone is doing us an injustice. But, after any emotional outburst, it's really important to calm down and get some perspective.

So, first, get some distance. Give yourself some thinking time so that you're absolutely clear about the situation – or what's going wrong. Get your diary, a few sheets of paper or your laptop and write it all down, as clearly as you can. Setting it down in black and white really helps you gain that perspective, and can let you vent your feelings, too. It can also be useful as a backup tool if any facts need to be brought up at a later stage!

It could be you've just been denied the opportunity to go on a training course at work, one which could really help you change your career. Or your employer won't give you the chance to extend your skills or further your experience. Your goal may be to get further qualifications, and perhaps your tutor is obstructing your progress in some way. Perhaps it's more personal – someone close to you is blocking your path – being negative and generally making life difficult for you. (Yes, been there.)

Whatever the specifics of your situation, start by stepping back and asking yourself, 'What is happening here?'

It helps to explore what's going on by answering questions such as:

- What am I feeling?

- Why do I feel like this?

- Why do I feel that person is obstructing me?

- What is motivating them? (e.g. jealousy, thinking you're a threat)

- To what extent could it be personal?

- So where am I now?

- Has this changed my outlook?

- How can I change how I feel?

- How can I change the situation I am in?

- Could it be that I have done something wrong here?

- Am I really seeing it clearly?

- What can I do to move beyond this situation?

It may also help to try to get into the other person's head: look at it from their vantage point. Ask yourself how it might seem to them. Perhaps the situation actually involves a third party? It could be there's a problem in the 'communication line' and coming out of somebody else's perception?

Only once you stand back and examine it from every angle can you establish the ways in which this person/conversation is obstructing you from your goal – and find your own solutions out of it.

Would it help to sit down and troubleshoot together? Could you open up the discussion by saying something along the lines of 'I've heard you've been told I have done such and such'? And then suggest, 'Actually, let me tell you how I see the chain of events'?

Sometimes people aren't given the opportunity to explain. It all happens so quickly. Even if the outcome isn't as you perhaps would have liked, at least you've had the chance to give an explanation, and confronting the issue can be a weight off your shoulders, at least.

Know Your Rights

It's always a good idea to do a bit of research if you feel someone is being obstructive, particularly in the work environment. For example, if your line manager isn't giving you time out to go on a certain course, when you notice colleagues around you do have that right, would it help to speak to someone in HR about what your job entitles you to do? Do you have the power of appeal if an exam or assessment doesn't go successfully? Perhaps your dream involves launching a new company or product, or getting planning permission to build something. Again, ask questions, stay informed.

Get a Team Behind You

Rallying a group of supportive people in your 'corner', who aren't directly involved in the situation, can also help you get perspective and provide the necessary backup. When I'd been failed on that pre-selection course, it really helped me to get the opinions of my colleagues on the course. (Their backup also gave me the courage to ask for time off to better my skills – which would also be useful to employers.)

Is there someone who can investigate the situation for you? Do you have some friends or colleagues who can stand up for you or just give you their support?

Be Obstinate, But Pick Your Battles ...

The first time I was unsuccessful on the Army PTI pre-selection course, I was able to stand back and acknowledge where I went wrong. There was no issue to fight against – the verdict was fair, I just needed to improve in certain skills. But the time I was on my PTI course was very clearly unacceptable – and wrong – and I was not going to stand back, and I was vindicated by being allowed back on the course after giving my side of the events.

All I can say is, keep focused: don't let anyone stand in the way of your goal, but at the same time keep a sense of fair play and your feet grounded in reality, too! Know when someone is obstructing you for good reason, and also when you may not be quite ready for the next step – what can you do to make progress?

... Always Remember: No One Person Controls Your Destiny

When you come across someone who seems determined to block your progress, it really does make you think he or she can destroy your ambition and progress – the dream itself. But you have to remember the person is just *one* person – and there are lots of different routes to where you want to go.

Always try look at things from every angle so that, instead of losing heart, you actually sharpen your resolve and remind yourself that, despite that person's influence or behaviour, there are other ways to reach success. You just need the time to work out how to bypass that person, and not let him or her ruin your dream.

And there's always, *always* a way.

Difficult Conversations: How to Have Them *and* Still Get What You Want

We all know that good communication skills can really help you move forward in life. They're particularly important when you find yourself in tricky situations with people, or when you need to make a break and move on. Also, change can be incredibly hard for those around us as well, so knowing how to handle situations firmly but sensitively can make all the difference.

When you're an athlete, you're constantly evolving and developing, and there comes a time when you might need to change the team of people around you. You may need to swap a certain team-member

– a coach or physio, for example – or find someone new who is able to take you to the next level. And time is all-important when you're an athlete – you have to get on with it. Everything is about *that* minute, *that* performance, so every decision really matters.

Even so, moving on can be tough, especially when it involves a particular person who has been a friend during your journey, or a coach who has spent a lot of time and has been committed to helping you achieve. It's horrible having to tell a valued team-member you need to make a change, because you don't want to hurt anyone, or make them feel they haven't been adequate. But the bottom line is you need to do what you think is right and necessary to help you move forward.

The first time I had do to it was with a great coach, Wes Duncan, in 1993. He's a brilliant guy, really lovely and still a friend now. He had brought me back into athletics when I'd taken time out during my Army career. But after only one year of training with him I thought, 'Wes is a great friend, but not the right coach for me *right now*.' I needed someone who had known me for a long time – as a junior, who knew my temperament, knew the way that I worked, understood my work ethic; someone who would know how to shape me.

I didn't know how to make the break, other than think carefully beforehand and talk from the heart. So I said something like this: 'I really respect everything you've done for me, but I feel that if I'm going to take this seriously, I need someone who knows me and has done so for a long time.' Fortunately Wes understood and accepted that, which was a real relief for me. So I got back with my coach Dave Arnold, who had trained me as a junior and who knew me inside-out. (Wes stayed on to do my massage and remained a key part of my team, and is now one of my closest friends.)

Dave and I worked together for many seasons after that (although we parted company for a while over a misunderstanding), and while we were working together I won eight medals, which was fantastic.

As I progressed and my goals changed, the time came for me to make another big change, and in 2002 I split with Dave again. Even though I'd won gold in the Commonwealth Games and bronze at the European Championships, there was something not quite right. I realised that my environment wasn't right for me – it wasn't giving me enough motivation, confidence or structure. I needed somewhere I could concentrate purely on athletics. I knew that if I wanted to be the athlete I'd dreamed of, I had to be very single-minded. So after much soul-searching

I ended up moving away from the UK, renting my house out and going to live in South Africa, and eventually leaving Dave and working with coach Margo Jennings.

I talked in Chapter 3 about Margo's great approach – she was level-headed, motivating, positive, and I just knew she was right for me at that time in my career. You know when you're making change for the right reasons. It just feels right inside, and that's when you have to make that leap, particularly if you're stuck in a rut. But of course another change meant another difficult conversation – I knew telling Dave was going to be tough.

Lots of people reading this book will face this kind of dilemma. Perhaps you want to move jobs and start a new career. This may involve leaving a boss who has been fantastic and supportive, and may feel like you're letting him or her down. Or you may want to move to a different part of the country – or the world – which may involve hurting the people you love and respect in the process. Perhaps you need to make a break from a working partnership in order to follow your new life direction. It may be you've teamed up with a 'weight loss buddy' who is always straying and trying to lead you astray, or a 'study buddy' who just isn't prepared to put in the hours that you are to get that degree. Perhaps you'd prefer to go it alone and create some distance between you? Or it may be that you're trying to start a new business with someone, but you can't see eye to eye on things, or he or she isn't quite the business partner you'd imagined. And so it may be time to move on.

These are all really hard decisions to make, and tricky conversations to have. So how do you do it?

Talking from the heart (without being personal or destructive) is one option. I remember saying to Dave, 'I'm 32 years old. You've known me since I was 12 and we've been through a lot. I'm not saying you won't be part of my life, but I need to make this drastic change. If I don't take this chance I think I'll regret it for the rest of my life, and I don't want to do that. I've got one more Olympics – it's only two years away and I need an environment which will give me the fire in my belly again.'

Of course it hurt Dave a lot, but I think he understood. And because he'd been so instrumental in my career and because I trusted him so much, he was the one I kept in constant text-contact with at the Olympic Games in 2004 – he was always there to reassure me. He may not have been my coach anymore, but for me he was that somebody we all need to keep us in that positive frame of mind and to keep us going.

So for anyone faced with a difficult conversation,

I'd say try to use the same careful preparation here as you have been doing elsewhere. *And always write it down first*; it helps you clarify what you want and why you may be making this difficult decision.

Here are the key questions to think about. Be prepared to listen, but also stick to your guns:

- Why do I need to make this change from this person/situation? (How will it help take me towards my goal?)

- How will that change affect this person? (Be prepared for how he or she will feel – perhaps you can anticipate possible responses.)

- What do I really want to say to this person? (What are my motives and how can I put those across sensitively but firmly?)

- What positive contributions has this person/ situation made to me? (Acknowledge their strengths.)

- Is there any compromise that we can reach? (That is, can I do this fairly, diplomatically?)

It may help to write out a few drafts of what you're going to say, or rehearse it to yourself first. Be clear about what you want to achieve so that the conversation stays focused.

And even though you may get nervous, feel sick or worry endlessly about the conversation, once you have done it, it will be a big weight off your shoulders!

OBSTACLE 2: DEALING WITH SETBACKS

These are inevitable on anyone's journey to success. The trick is not to let setbacks and disappointments beat you or sway you from your direction. Being resilient and staying positive are the only ways to get through them. And there are also some good ways to 'manage your thinking'.

For me, the biggest (and ongoing) setbacks in my athletics career were injuries.

I started getting my first injuries back in 1996, with a really painful stress fracture in my shin. I first noticed a small bruise as I flew over to Tallahassee, Florida for the British team holding camp, but over the next couple of days it became incredibly painful. When I was diagnosed with a stress fracture I was gutted. It was the year of the Olympics, in fact only two weeks before they started and my very first Olympic Games, too – so it was an emotional time. I remember thinking, 'Here I am at the Olympic Games, but I have a stress fracture. I was in the best shape of my life. But now I can't do my final preparation, and I'm *in pain*.'

During the Games, the doctor had to give me really painful anti-inflammatory injections in my shin before each race in order to numb the pain. Somehow (though I don't know how) I made it through the heats and semi-finals, but I do remember sobbing uncontrollably when the needle scratched the bone in my leg – the pain and emotional strain were too much.

Despite this I still managed to come fourth in the 800m final, which was amazing given what my body was going through! In fact it was probably that tiny negative voice in my head reminding me that I was running *with an injury* that actually lost me the bronze medal in the end! In fact, despite the injury, I came out of that year fired up, thinking, 'I know I can do better. I know I *will* do better one year.'

In the middle of 1997 I was 5 seconds faster than anyone else in the world. Getting a British record – after breaking a really longstanding record – left me feeling on top of the world. I was going into the World Championships as a favourite, it was all fantastic. But then my world crashed again when I ended up rupturing my calf and tearing my Achilles tendon in the heats (the first round). It was like another kick in the guts.

It took me a long time to get over that – and I just about got back on form in time for the Commonwealth Games in 1998, in which I won the silver medal and which kept up my belief that I was good enough.

But the next bitter blow came at the end of 1999 when I fell ill with glandular fever. I had the worst season competitively of my whole career, and to add to the disappointment I became injured yet again at the beginning of 2000 – another Olympics year.

It was horrendous. I had damaged my back in a cross-country race, which ended up affecting the femoral nerve running down my right leg. For five months I lost all feeling in my leg from the hip to the knee, and it created knock-on problems including a tear in my right calf muscle. As an athlete you simply have to adapt your training around an injury – so I did cardio work on gym equipment such as the stepper, rowing machine and the bike, and trained in the pool every day. But despite my determination I would still cry myself to sleep at night, thinking I would never fulfil my dreams.

And yet I'd always had that belief that I was good enough, and had always given it my all in training. So when I came across an obstacle – in this case my injury – I started to ask myself, 'Should I be moving through this? Am I strong enough? Good enough?' As an athlete your mindset is critical to your performance. So I had to decide how I would *mentally* approach this massive setback. I remember saying to myself, 'OK I am not going through that again – I am not going to come back from the Games without a medal, as I did in '96.' I was aware that, at 30, this could be my last Olympics – with all my dreams potentially going out of the window.

During that six-month build-up prior to the Games, I held on tightly to that mindset. I would repeat to myself, 'I am going to get over this injury, I am going to beat it, and I am going to get to those Games.' It was just that kind of passion I needed psychologically to help me get through the injury. It really helped me to focus on what I was going to achieve rather than dwell on the struggle and trauma I was facing. I took it day by day, but I just kept looking ahead.

How on earth I managed to qualify for and reach those Games I will never know – because, realistically – with the lack of running I had done – I shouldn't have made it! I had only been running properly for six weeks prior to those Games, but once I got there I knew I had to make the most of it.

Getting through to the semi-finals was amazing, and you can imagine how I felt on reaching the final – and winning the bronze medal! I couldn't believe it.

Again, perhaps the only reason I didn't get silver or win was because of that doubt, that little voice saying, 'I shouldn't be here.' But given everything I had been through, that bronze was like a gold medal to me.

You can see what I mean when I talk about the rollercoaster ride I was on. I knew the calibre of athlete I was, I knew the standard I had reached, and I knew I was 100 per cent committed. None of that was in question. It was my body holding me back, and therefore out of my control. Incredibly frustrating.

So that's why I understand what it feels like to encounter problems along the way.

You may be following your path, treading a really careful line, when circumstances in your life put you back one step. It's really easy when things go wrong to want to give up.

Whatever you do, *don't do that*. I worked through my setbacks, and so can you. Work out how you're going to deal with that setback, almost grieve about it, sort it out in your mind, put it behind you or forget it before you can move forward again. You need to keep a rational head on your shoulders, however emotional you may be feeling.

- Get perspective – ask yourself to what extent this setback or disappointment is really stopping your progress? Remind yourself it is probably only a temporary setback. And it's not the end of the world. You really will get through it.

- Re-examine your timeline or flowchart: it might help to ask yourself, 'What could I have done differently? Where did I go off-track? Do I need a reality check here? Shall I adjust my vision and make it more realistic?'

- Boost your confidence about where you are now: what has been going well? Acknowledge your successes up to this point.

- Ask yourself, 'In what positive ways am I nearer my goal?' Again, you're aiming to reinforce to yourself that you *can* do this. You can reach your goal.

- What do you need to do differently now? Devise ways to get yourself out of your rut, or sit down and troubleshoot some realistic solutions to your problems. (Another opinion is always useful here, so talk to a trusted friend or colleague, or an expert who is prepared to offer advice.)

- What can you do today that can push you forward again? Doing something *now*, however small, and getting back into action really helps you feel you're back in control.

- Remind yourself that this setback is not going to stop you ... Switch on that encouraging voice in your head and repeat it to yourself often. It helped me to repeat positive statements to myself. (Revisit Chapter 3 for some useful mindsets.)

OBSTACLE 3: MAKING DIFFICULT DECISIONS

How good are you at making decisions? How confident are you that the choices you're making are the right ones? What do you do when life is potentially leading you to two, or maybe three, different paths? How do you respond when you've been working towards your goal and suddenly you find yourself pulled off-course – by a person, or by circumstances? How do you know the right way to go?

I talk a lot about how important it is to me to avoid living with those nagging 'if onlys'. In fact, the prospect of having regrets has been one of my greatest motivators. Choices are part of life, and we can all find ourselves at a crossroads, faced with decisions about which way to turn. Sometimes the choices are straightforward, easy. Sometimes those decisions can be big, life-changing ones.

One of the hardest decisions I ever had to make was when I was 24. It was 1994, I was in the Army, still hoping to join the Physical Training Corps. Alongside this, I had just won two prestigious international medals – Gold at the Commonwealth Games in 1994 (1,500m) and Silver at the European Championships (1,500m). To be honest, I had achieved these without giving a full 100 per cent to my training, so I was left wondering what more I could achieve if I really gave my all to my athletics. It was an exciting time. The World Championships were taking place later that year, in August 1995, and I was hoping I'd be selected for them.

Meanwhile, I still had an Army career to focus on. I had already deferred the date for my PTI training course after passing that horrendous selection, and now it was confirmed that the deferred date would be early 1995. It was a huge choice. All I'd ever wanted to be was a PTI, but if I did another six-month training course, I knew I wouldn't have enough left in me to run at my best. After lots of discussion with my coach Dave, and the officers in charge at Aldershot, we agreed that I could defer going on the course for a second time. This meant that I could train for the Championships but could also complete my PTI training afterwards. It was a good solution.

It was a great learning experience at the Gothenburg World Championships. I didn't win the 1,500 metres (even though I went in thinking I could), but I did win bronze in the 800 metres – and came home elated! And there was further success to celebrate later on that year, at the Grand Prix finals in Monaco, when I slashed the British record in a time of 1:56.21 (a record which I am proud to say still stands today as I write this book).

Walking back into life in barracks was always strange after the highs and lows on the track and the excitement of international events. And this time I came back with the ultimate decision to make: what would take priority in my life now? My running or my Army career?

The moment had come when I had to make that tough choice – should I accept or turn down my place on the PTI course? Bear in mind that no one ever turns down a place on that course – they're like gold dust. But I knew that if I committed myself totally to the intense training that would be required to get me to the Olympics (1996), then I would have to forgo my place. If I wanted to get selected to run for Great Britain, I would have to give 100 per cent to my athletics training. It would be impossible to do both.

Believe me, it was a tough dilemma – both of these meant so much to me. But after much soul-searching I knew which way I would go: my achievements in athletics during that year had made me realise how strongly I held my Olympic dream. Deep down I knew that I couldn't let it go ...

As it was, there was a great solution to this dilemma. When I approached my commanding officer, Lieutenant Colonel McCord, to discuss my options, she was really sympathetic. We discussed various possibilities, and eventually decided I could be transferred to the Army Youth Team based in Mill Hill. It was a fantastic direction to go in – a really rewarding role where I would help kids get the best out of themselves – and it meant I could still do my athletics. It was a win–win situation. Of course there was a certain sadness at not moving forward as a PTI, but I was on to great new challenges, which really spurred me on and kept me looking forward ...

Looking back, I had always thought that my career in the Army was important – but in time I realised that I wanted to fulfil my second dream. I suppose the moment came when I knew where my destiny lay.

The rest is history, of course. So it all turned out better than I could ever have wished. And I will always know that my decisions were right ...

It's one thing to wonder what the future might have held for you if you had made different decisions. But *not* doing anything at all because you are unable to make these kinds of big decisions is another thing!

How to Make Choices: Decisions by Numbers

This is a simple exercise, but it always works:

If you're faced with two or three big choices – or need to identify what's really important to you – start by writing each option down on paper.

Then slowly and carefully dissect the implications of each one.

Start by thinking: 'What will happen if I choose option number one?' For example, your dilemma might go something like this: 'What will happen if I go on that training course at work which could really open up my horizons, but which I know my line manager doesn't really want me to go on?'

Or it could be along these lines: 'I really want to join that new running club but it meets on Thursdays – the same day as the regular weekly curry night with my friends.'

These are simple examples. But the idea is to consider your options from every angle. Write them down. Weigh everything up. Work out what's important to you. Stop making excuses.

While you're doing this, ask yourself, 'What's the worst that can happen here?' For example, 'If I accept that place on the training course, my line manager will be pretty tough on me once I get back to the office, and work might be unpleasant for a while' or 'I'll miss out on a great social time with my friends if I give up the curry night to sign up to the running club.' Really explore what you're worried about. How bad is it really?

Also ask yourself, 'What's the best that could happen?' It could be, 'Actually, I could persuade my line manager that I'll really benefit from this extra course, and show that I'm still really committed to my role and the department' or 'We could see if we're able to reschedule the weekly curry evening, which would mean I could do both.'

I think the key is really to focus on each angle. Ultimately, find out – and opt for – what matters most to you in your life. 'If I don't go on that training course I'll have to wait for another six months before the next one, and may not get the chance next time.' Decision made. Or 'Joining that running club is just what I need to move ahead with my running. I know it could give me the incentive I need to take this new fitness regime seriously.'

Once you start thinking about your options and writing them down, everything really does become clearer. It also helps you become more honest with yourself about what may be holding you back (i.e. just a lot of excuses!).

Time-frame It

Here's another good route to decision-making, as recommended by life coaches. For each dilemma you face, think about the implications of that action (or inaction) in these different time-spans:

- today
- in one year
- in five years.

For example, let's look at the running club vs curry night example again – perhaps you don't like to commit to that running club meeting on Thursdays because you know how much you and your friends value that curry evening – it's your one chance to all get together and, without it, you might all drift apart.

To what extent are you going to cause grief and upset by not being part of it anymore? What's the long-term ripple effect of this choice? Perhaps *today* they may feel disappointed that you've made this decision. But in a year's time will it all be worth it? Surely it won't mean the end of your friendship? Examine to what extent you are willing to go to compromise your own ambitions.

For example, going on that great training course might put your boss' nose out of joint for a week or so, but if it really propels you forward in your new venture it may be totally worth it one year and 10 years in the future. (Even if in the meantime, you have to endure the cold shoulder for a bit!)

It works with small stuff, too. If you can't decide whether or not to go to your exercise class tonight, think about how you'll feel about missing it – tomorrow, or next week, or even in a year's time. If skipping it is likely to lead you on a downward spiral back to the pub and out of the fitness routine altogether, then force yourself to head for the gym (you'll feel better once you do – guaranteed). If you can honestly say that a night off won't have any knock-on effects on your willpower or fitness levels, and isn't going to worry you – then take the evening off. It's about weighing up the consequences – and assessing the *lasting impact* of your decision.

Sometimes our plans and hopes do make us unpopular. Thinking about the impact a decision may have on others (or on your own dreams) – *now*, in *a year's time*, and in *five years* – is a really good way of gauging what's most important to you (and where you want to be in the future).

OBSTACLE 4: CHANGING YOUR PLANS

Plans, plans, plans. Athletes live their lives according to a strict training schedule. Your race plan is scheduled minutely on a day-to-day or week-to-week, month-to-month basis. It's your bible. That's why at the beginning of this book we talked about the importance of making this kind of carefully organised plan for your own particular goal. Breaking everything down into small step-by-step chunks helps you inch nearer your goal.

But sometimes it can all go wrong. Something crops up that throws that fantastic plan out the window. What do you do then?

As an athlete you may get a cold, or a niggle with your Achilles tendon, or some other unforeseen thing happens. That's when you need to sit down with your coach and make some serious changes to the schedule. For example, when I was injured and not able to run during training sessions, we just had to adapt my schedule around that. Sometimes I wasn't physically able to run at all! And I knew I had to work as hard in the pool or gym to simulate what I should have been doing out on the track. Athletes often have to shift entire weeks of training plans around, and if they're having to eliminate certain areas of training, they need to substitute them with something else. In your mind you still have to see it as training. You have to realise you're still on the right journey – you may not get there as quickly, but you'll still get there. Athletes who don't adapt lose out at the end of the day.

So when I wasn't fit enough to compete in the European Championships in 1998, I felt disappointed, as that was what I had trained for. Instead I had to move my ambitions beyond that to another goal – and the fact I had the Commonwealth Games to go for later in the year kept me going. It gave me that feeling of 'all is not yet lost!'

And that's the message I'd recommend when your plans get interrupted – for whatever reason. Remember, they're not carved in stone. Tell yourself, 'I'm in a really tough situation here, but I've got to get over this hurdle and the emotions that go with it. There's nothing I can do about things I cannot control, but there *is* something I can do to get myself to the next stage. It's time to alter my plans.'

It's like going for that dream job and not getting it. Some people get demoralised after the first failed interview. They blame themselves, think they're not good enough, or they find something that the interviewers did wrong or criticise how they acted. That's when you have to switch off that negative voice and get some constructive inner dialogue going on. You have to remind yourself that there were plenty of people going for that job, and that you don't know what the interviewers were after. You have to remind yourself of the fact that you may not have fitted the bill that time, but that does *not* mean you never will.

There will be another interview, something else to strive for. And you need to set to work planning for that one instead.

When you're re-evaluating your plans, it's also important to review yourself. Be self-critical and prepared to take on criticism. If it's a job or an exam, ask those in charge to give you feedback on how you performed. But also ask yourself, 'What could I have done better?' Did you express yourself well, turn up on time, do your research beforehand and dress appropriately? 'What didn't I know that I can find out about for next time?' If the answer is 'nothing,' then just look onwards and upwards. But there is always something to improve on.

Try not to be phased by the knockback. The key is to remember – with anything – just why you are doing it in the first place, which is generally because you were not happy as you were. Try not to let this, a small obstacle or hurdle, make you give it all up. Put it behind you – look at it in isolation, as just a bad day or a mere blip in your grand plan. Get back in the saddle, rework your plan, and switch into that positive mindset again.

- **Constantly review and adapt your goal 'flowchart'** (look back at Chapter 1 for ideas on this). The key is to remember that nothing

is carved in stone. Who knows, you may even
fine-tune your big goal – perhaps after a series
of knock-backs at job interviews you realise
that you'd prefer to go self-employed instead?
How do you work on that new direction? Or
perhaps it was too ambitious to try to lose 7lb
by the summer, given everything else going on
in your life. Adapting to your circumstances
means you will still get there, but your route
may be slightly more 'scenic'. Never be worried
about slowing down – it doesn't matter how
slow your progress is. As long as you keep going,
you'll get there.

- **Be your own critic.** By that I don't mean
  becoming a negative or destructive voice.
  Instead, give yourself honest appraisals of your
  performance/attitude/energy. Are you doing
  everything you can to stick to your goal? If
  something goes wrong, examine what happened
  there. To what extent could you have prevented
  it? What can you do now to stay on track?
  Keeping in touch with how you feel and how it's
  all going helps you stay focused.

- **Canvas outside opinions:** any good advice is
  valuable, and sometimes you need a different
  perspective. Try chatting through your

progress with someone you know who is a great motivator, or an expert in his or her field. Finding someone who can act as a mentor can help you offload your frustrations and boost your confidence.

OBSTACLE 5: HITTING ROCK BOTTOM

The problem with obstacles – whether that comes down to negative circumstances or people, or just flagging motivation (which we'll look at in the next chapter) – is that they can often drag you on a massive downward spiral. And before you know it you're feeling really despondent, depressed and worthless. At rock bottom.

I know. I've been there.

It happened in 2003, when a series of injuries that seemed never-ending threatened to destroy my Olympic dream for good. I really did find myself in the depths of despair. There was just one year until the Olympic Games, and yet I was going through injury yet again (for the seventh year running). As an athlete who devotes everything to running and winning, I felt panicky, as though I was running out of time. I was also emotionally exhausted, and everything was beginning to overwhelm me.

At the time I had recently starting training with Maria Mutola under her coach Margo, and I had been really enjoying my new programme. It was all looking so promising. But within weeks I got iliotibial band friction syndrome – an excruciating pain caused when the iliotibial band rubs against the knee joint. I tried to carry on training, but ended up over-compensating and overworking my right leg, and damaging my right calf.

Despite some great physiotherapy and sessions with a fantastic chiropractor, treatment was a long drawn-out process, and every step I took was agony. Around me, fellow athletes were training hard and seeing results. I just remember the pain and frustration of not being able to train.

My lowest point came when we all went to France for high-altitude training, to a mountain resort in the Pyrenees called Font Romeu. While Maria Mutola's training went from strength to strength, my injury kept me training in the pool. They were desperate times, and the pain, frustration and anxiety overwhelmed me. I felt cursed, and unable to cope with the bitter disappointment again. I really reached a dark place – somewhere I never want to return to!

I will not go into detail in this book, as it is in my autobiography, but how did I get out of that place? I knew I needed help, but I also knew no one could really work on those negative feelings but me. Looking back, time helped to a certain extent. As my leg gradually responded to treatment, I felt a bit more coherent. But the feelings of desperation took a lot longer to dispel.

I ended up speaking to a local doctor whom I met when we all moved to a training camp in St Moritz. That really helped. I had originally gone to see her for some massage, but ended up letting it all out. Just talking it through with an independent person who wouldn't judge me, who only looked at the here and now and not the baggage, allowed me to offload all my anxieties. She helped me see that it was my deep frustration about not being able to fulfil this powerful desire within me that was leading me to desperate acts.

The doctor recommended some medication to help lift my mood, but suggested herbal remedies to raise my serotonin levels – as I thought anti-depressants might come under the IAAF's (International Amateur Athletics Federation) list of banned drugs, which as an athlete is of course a big no-no. Talking confidentially about how I felt inside – of the struggle of being up and down emotionally and the expectations I had of myself, helped me so much. Along with the tablets (which were chocolate flavoured – another good thing!) and the fact my legs continued to make good progress with the treatment, I managed to drag myself out of that pit of despair. But I can honestly say it was the hardest and worst time of my life!

So what have I learned from that experience? First, that we all have the potential to lose our way sometimes. However confident you are, continual knockbacks can drag you down unless you find a way to deal with those emotions along the way. It's really hard when you feel you can't talk to anyone about it or don't want to worry other people – but don't suffer alone.

Above all, you need remember this is how you are *feeling*, this is not *fact*. There is a way out. Keep focused on what you are trying to achieve, and make sure you work through *why* you have reached such a low point.

Try to stay positive. The light at the end of the tunnel can be brighter than ever before!

Move Up from Rock Bottom

- **Find an independent person you can confide in**. Talking to someone outside your circle really helps. Don't try to go it alone. Talk to your GP or an independent counsellor.

- **Take one day at a time:** instead of looking ahead in panic, thinking 'There's so much to do, I'm doomed to fail that exam,' or 'I'll never lose weight or get fit, or get a great job, or make any change in my life' – try to switch to a lower gear. Moving your horizons nearer, and taking one small step at a time, are vital when you're feeling overwhelmed by the bigger picture. So when you're really low, try to do something small from your list. When you can tick it off, remind yourself, 'I'm on my way.' Small victories will get you there, little by little. *That's how I survived those weeks. It was an uphill battle, but I made it. And even though I was not in the best frame of mind for the World Championships, I still ended up getting a silver medal. So I changed it round dramatically. And, honestly, so can you.*

- **Gather your supporters:** having a group of people around who are always encouraging is so important. Try to spend time with positive people; it rubs off. In Chapter 2 we talked about gathering together your own team. This team is even more important when you're going through a bad patch, or when you feel you're destined to fail. People who care about you can give you a shoulder to cry on, or some good advice, or motivate you again.

- **Look after yourself.** When you're at rock bottom, you tend to neglect yourself. But if you're not getting enough sleep, or not eating properly, or not taking any time out to relax, your energy levels are going to be low and your mood isn't going to improve. Make an effort to look after yourself – and treat yourself, too. Every day, take time to do something fun or that makes you happy, or distracts you from your feelings. Treating yourself well is a sign that you're a worthwhile person.

WHAT TO DO TODAY FOR SUCCESS TOMORROW

✓ *Get some perspective on difficult people or setbacks.* How bad are they really? Writing about the impact they may be having on your progress is a useful way to clarify your situation, and work out what you need to do to move beyond them.

✓ *Tweak your flowchart plan according to your new challenges or setbacks*. Having a brand new revised plan can motivate you again.

✓ *Remind yourself what you have achieved so far.* Congratulate yourself on those successes – it shows that, in spite of the problems, you are moving in the right direction.

✓ *Be good to yourself.* Taking the time to eat and sleep well, spending time with positive people and treating yourself occasionally are really important for your overall well-being.

CHAPTER 5

Motivation Secrets: How to Tap into Your Willpower

'No one stays motivated 100 per cent of the time. You'll have good days and you'll have bad days. The trick is to keep that image of your own success so crystal clear in your head that nothing can keep you from it ...'

– Kelly

Following a dream is never easy. It requires energy, enthusiasm and drive. And sometimes it's hard to keep that level of commitment going.

So what happens when it starts to feel too much like hard work? What if the novelty begins to wear off? Perhaps it gets harder to see results, or you don't see results quickly enough – you may reach a plateau with your weight loss or fitness. If your goal is to get further qualified, you may find that the revision or essay-writing just get boring. Or maybe the success you dreamed of isn't coming quickly enough.

Chances are there's nothing specific or major getting in your way (no big, external obstacles like the ones we looked at in the last chapter). But somehow you're losing the energy for it all. You don't have the same drive you started with. You're losing your motivation and you don't know how to get it back.

This chapter is about finding a way to be excited again, and getting back on track.

Over the years a lot of people have asked me, 'How do you motivate yourself? What keeps you going?' To tell you the truth, a lot of it simply comes down to my personality. If I want something, I go after it and I tend not to stop until I get it. (And if I don't get what I was hoping for, at least I can say I tried.) I've always been like that. It's who I am, and I can't change it or think differently.

It sums up my philosophy, really, which is this: why go through life moaning about wanting to do something without at least *trying* to get it? Why remain unhappy with your situation without at least doing something to *try* to change it? Wishing for something without following it up with action, but then being unhappy and frustrated about it, just doesn't make sense to me. To me, there's nothing worse than living with regrets.

I'm a very driven person by nature, but I know not everybody is. Mind you, being constantly fired up can have its drawbacks. Sometimes it's exhausting being me – and it's exhausting for everyone else around me! I get frustrated. I remember when I celebrated – or do I mean commiserated? – turning 39 +1 (I have a hang-up about age). All I could think is, 'There's so much out there I still want to do, I don't want to run out of time!'

It's ridiculous, really. 'Look at what you have done with your life,' everyone tells me. I know they're right, but for some reason I want to learn more, achieve more – I don't ever want to have that 'if only' feeling.

However, even naturally driven people like me have days when it's all too much. Believe me, I certainly know what it's like to feel shattered and want to lie on the sofa all evening with some chocolate! As an athlete you also have to summon up energy and motivation, often training twice a day, six days a week. There are days when everything aches! You are running early in the morning and have a track session later in the evening, when the last thing you want to do is get out there in the freezing cold or in the snow!

There were so many times I'd dread my training because I knew how painful it was going to be. (I dreaded the excruciating stomach cramps that I got after a hard track session – it would leave me feeling sick and doubled up in pain for at least 40 minutes.) And I also had to put up with constant restrictions on my diet – as an athlete you're only as good as the food you put in your body, so you have to be really firm with yourself. Imagine having to watch what you eat *all the time*. Chinese takeaways and chocolate were strictly once-a-week treats when I was training. (And for a chocoholic like me, that's hard. Really hard.)

That's why I understand it when people say they have problems staying motivated. It can be really tough when your energy plummets and your resolve weakens halfway through. But I strongly believe it *is* possible to regain that momentum. So all I'm saying is, don't give up now! All is not lost!

Personally, I think that when people say they have problems with motivation, it comes down to one of three main reasons:

- When people say they're not motivated a lot of the time, I suspect it comes back to *not knowing what it is they really want*. You need a *reason* to be motivated. You need to know what your efforts will bring you in terms of rewards. And that is why all the exercises in Chapter 1 are so important – the ones that help you establish what it is that makes you happy or fulfilled, and help you to *define* your goals. Establishing this is a fundamental stage. So in this chapter we're going to go back over some of those areas, and kickstart that initial process.

- The second reason for flagging motivation? Let's call them 'off-days' – which everyone has, however focused they may be on their goal. You may still believe in what you're trying to achieve, but may have lost that initial drive which keeps you fighting for it. People who are trying to lose weight may be familiar with this – you have one bad day when you overindulge, then you feel guilty or it leads to another one, then you may gain some weight, become discouraged and end up wanting to give up. You still *want* to lose weight, tone up, get fit and feel good about yourself again, but you feel you're back to square one. Oh, I know all about 'off-days'. An athlete goes through incredibly frustrating days – perhaps training doesn't go well and you don't reach your targets. You lose a race – or lots of races! You get a cold or a bug. Bad days happen to everyone.

- The third key reason people lose motivation is that *they lose confidence in themselves,* and it makes the challenge ahead look just too daunting. You may know what you want, you may have been really focused on it, but perhaps you're losing confidence in your own ability to see it through.

So here's how I would recommend addressing these three key issues.

GET BACK IN TOUCH WITH YOURSELF

Do I Still Want This?

The first exercise is to work out how you're feeling about your goal right now. The bottom line is you can't feel motivated about a project or an idea unless you know what it's going to bring you in terms of ultimate rewards. In order to have something to be motivated about, you need to know *why* you're pursuing it.

That's why, as an athlete, I battled through my off-days and through the really, really hard times, and yet stayed motivated. I *knew* what I wanted – I wanted to win. I was after those amazing feelings of achievement. I wanted to push myself to the limits, to be the best I could be. The best in the world.

So now is the time to define what it means to *you* to achieve *your* particular goal. Start by having another look at the goals you set yourself earlier on in the book, and check that they are still what you really want and are realistic. Remind yourself why you're on this new journey. Here are some useful questions to ask yourself:

- *Why did I want to do it in the first place? How is it going to make me happy?*

- *How will achieving it make me feel? How is it going to enhance my life?*

- *Is this still what I want? Will it still make me feel good about myself and fulfill me? Will it make me healthier? Improve my lifestyle?*

- *How will pursuing this help me move away from the feelings of frustration or unhappiness or lack of fulfilment I have been living with? How will it change my life and bring me what I want?*

Spend some time on this exercise. You need to see the end result, start living it in your mind, to get fired up all over again. It really helps to visualise what you want again – imagine yourself achieving it – the satisfaction you will feel when you reach the end of your journey. Really focus on the great feelings of achievement that will come with it ...

Hopefully this will re-ignite that spark and get you excited again.

Be aware, too, that you may simply have decided that the goal you initially wanted to pursue isn't for you after all – that new career, or the new sport, or that business idea – perhaps you've reached a certain stage and realise they aren't going to bring you the satisfaction you anticipated. Perhaps it's really not as achievable as you originally thought. That's fine. If you genuinely feel you need to change your goal – then change it. But be sure it's for the right reasons.

WHY AM I LOSING MOTIVATION?

This is where you try to work out *why* you may have lost your initial drive. Here are some useful questions to ask yourself:

Is It Too Hard?

Have you taken on too much, too soon? Do you need to alter your timeline? If you set your goals too high, you'll get disheartened. So, re-examining your timelines – making sure you're setting yourself realistic goals within a realistic timeframe – is really important.

Am I Juggling Too Much?

This is an issue I see a lot among the 'On Camp with Kelly' athletes that I mentor. They're incredibly motivated young people, but sometimes it can all get on top of them. Occasionally they get down or discouraged by their athletics performance, but a lot of that comes down to the fact they're juggling so many things. They may be applying to university, studying for exams, looking for a job, and alongside this they're having to focus on their athletics and train twice a day. Not surprisingly, they find it increasingly difficult to stay motivated every minute of the day.

Am I Feeling Overwhelmed?

Could it be you're trying to do too many things at once, on your own? Make a list of everything you have going on in your life at the moment. Ask yourself if there's just too much on your shoulders to give you the space and time to focus on your goal. Think about how you could shift your schedule or commitments around to make room for your new project.

How Am I Feeling Physically?

Tired? Unwell? Stressed with work and home life? When I was training, having a cold or a niggle somewhere in my body, having to cope with an issue going on in my home life or just not having enough sleep – any of these would really have an impact on my performance, my energy levels and my emotions.

If that sounds familiar, then you need a day off! Don't ignore what your body is trying to tell you. Sometimes it's fine to take a step back.

Do I Have Enough Small Targets to Keep Me Going?

Little targets are really motivating. Seeing *progress* is really motivating. That's why athletes break everything down and focus on that day, that moment, that performance. And that's why breaking your goal down into different stages, and charting your progress in your diary, is such a good idea. You can see yourself moving in the right direction. If you only ever look to the end result, the ultimate goal may seem completely out of reach and like a huge mountain to climb, instead of a gradual incline that's manageable and progressive. Ticking off smaller achievements is empowering. That sense of satisfaction on passing milestones really propels you forward.

Do I Have Enough Support?

I keep talking about the importance of gathering around you a group of supporters, because from my experience I realise how crucial this is to your overall success. So hopefully all the members in 'Team You' are doing all they can to help you (see Chapter 2 to review your team!). If not, now is the time to have another chat and explain what kind of extra input you may need from them. With too much on your plate you won't have the enthusiasm, let alone the time, to follow a new project through. Ask yourself who could help free you up or take on some of your commitments in the short term? Who can you turn to for some inspiring words of wisdom to get you back on track?

Do I Know Everything I Need to Know?

When you're going in a totally new life direction – you need as much information as possible. Sometimes the thought of all you need to know can be overwhelming and can put you off before you get very far. (My head was spinning when I first started looking into the business world with the intention of setting up my own company. I needed to take on board how it all works in order to do it properly. It was pretty daunting at first – a world away from athletics!) But you must always be willing to learn, however scary that may seem. Take it slowly, digesting bits of information little by little rather than jumping straight in, and gradually it will start to make sense. Ultimately, the more knowledgeable you are, the more confident you'll become.

Five Components of Motivation that Helped Me Achieve Ultimate Success: Direction, Intensity, Persistence, Continuity and Performance

Direction (e.g. goal setting, specific events, times)

I had a goal/dream when I was 14 to be an Olympic champion. To get there was a long process of club, county, national, international and eventually world class races over a 20-year period. I had to race at the highest level, winning the 800m in 1:56.38 and the 1500m in 3:57.9.

Intensity (e.g. the amount of effort and energy required)

As a senior athlete I had to train very intensely. During my senior career I trained twice a day, six days a week, with one rest day a week – training sessions consisted of weights, circuit training, pool running, long runs, track work of speed and speed endurance, and hill running.

Persistence

In training you have to work to your maximum ability to enable you to fulfil your potential and also to be among the best in the world; the problem is you risk a lot of injuries, like I did.

Continuity (e.g. the motivation to keep training for so many years)

Continuity is very important, so the biggest challenge to my motivation was when I suffered injuries, as I had to maintain my fitness with all of the above training without running!

Performance (relationship between motivation and performance)

I believe that 80 per cent of your performance comes from natural self-belief (as long as you have the ability and have trained well). The ultimate single factor that motivated me in the pursuit of achieving my goals was the desire to become an Olympic champion.

BOOSTING MOTIVATION

Hopefully the exercises above have helped you to identify a few of the reasons why you sometimes find it hard to stay motivated. Now, here are some good ways to keep you inspired and boost your willpower.

Buddy Up

Joining forces with like-minded people is a really good way to refuel that enthusiasm. Having a weight-loss buddy or someone to go running with, or teaming up with someone to work on a new business plan with you, means you have someone on hand to offer support and encouragement. You can share ideas and spur each other on. Joining a club, such as a running club, or going on a particular course – anything that gives you the chance to spend time with other motivated people with similar goals – can be really inspiring.

It's also worth canvassing the opinions of people you respect or who have excelled in the field you're pursuing, to give you feedback on your ideas and progress. When I was researching business plans and working out how to develop my ideas, I sought help and advice from as many influential people as I could.

People are often willing to share their expertise with others. Sometimes you need one spark, or some brilliant piece of advice from someone in the know to give you stimulation! Having an outside expert who is able to give you a structured plan of how to move forward can be invaluable. Be willing to learn, and don't be afraid to ask questions.

Just Do 10 Minutes

On those low-energy days it's really hard to muster the enthusiasm for anything, let alone a new challenge. Those are the days when it's easy to skip your workout or abandon your revision or interview preparation. Take a tip from nutrition experts, who often say that a good way to handle a craving is to distract yourself for 10 minutes – keep busy until the yearning passes. This '10-minute' concept could be a good route to get you motivated, too. For example, just tell yourself you'll spend just 10 minutes exercising, or doing your business figures, or practising that presentation – or whatever it is you're putting off. Chances are you'll get immersed in what you're doing and you'll end up doing a lot more than 10 minutes. Plus you'll feel great that you actually achieved something ...

Get Techno-support

There is so much material out there on the internet these days. It can be a great source of information – and motivation. One scientific study showed that just getting regular email support can make people more successful in their ventures! This study, on a group of dieters (published in the *Archives of Internal Medicine*) found that the ones who signed up to an online weight-loss programme and who received information, tips and supportive messages via email, lost more weight than other dieters. It may be worth signing up to an online programme that offers this kind of feedback and guidance. Or just ask a friend or one of your 'Team You' members to send you regular words of encouragement via email!

Change Your Thinking, Change Your Language

Instead of saying, 'I can't,' start saying 'I can' – or at the very least, 'I am going to try ...' Rather than focusing on 'problems', instead see them as 'challenges': this just gives them a more positive spin. Stop thinking of things you need to do as a chore – 'Urgh, I must do this' or 'I have to do that', and think of them as things you have *chosen* to do or you *want* because they are going to take you a step nearer to what you are striving for. For every negative you give yourself, try to offer yourself a positive instead.

Above all, try not to stay in the past. Don't listen to that little voice in your head that says you can't. If you're trying to shape up, for example, tell yourself that it was the approach to weight loss that failed you on your previous attempts – it wasn't right, or too strict, or not realistic. Ban all talk of 'dieting' – it's such a negative and short-term concept. (Instead, be specific and constructive: 'I want to tone up,' 'I have only 4lb to lose to reach my optimum weight,' 'I need to be stronger.') In the same way, remind yourself that the jobs you were chasing weren't right for you *at that time* (but that, now, your attitude, knowledge, etc. are much sharper). It's about giving yourself a pep talk so that you become able to give yourself a positive focus instead.

Take Time Out

As I have said before, I'm a firm believer in taking time out when it all gets too much. In the Army, that wasn't really an option for me – you couldn't head off somewhere when your drills or being on exercise all became a bit tough and exhausting. You had to see it through. And as an athlete you certainly couldn't skip that week's training, or tell your coach you were going back to bed because you felt a bit worn out.

(Never having had the choice *not* do something may be one reason why I stay motivated – giving up hasn't been an option.)

But nowadays I do just that – I take time out to clear my head, spend time with friends, turn off my computer and tell myself I'll come back to it a bit later when my head's not spinning and I've had some 'me time'. So taking a little time to reflect, or a day away from it, isn't the end, it's just that – a day off.

Think 'Failure' ...

When the urge to give it all up and abandon your goal creeps up on you, try picturing yourself having done just that – having given up on your dream, not trying any more – and feeling sad, regretful and frustrated as a result. According to psychology experts, picturing the negative consequences of giving up on hopes and aspirations can actually be a really powerful motivator and an effective way to kickstart your enthusiasm. A study published in the *British Journal of Health Psychology* on people who had set themselves exercise plans found that those who focused on the feelings of disappointment and regret that they would experience if they abandoned their workouts were actually more likely to carry on with their fitness goals. Sometimes it may pay to 'think negative'!

Inspired by Sound

One scientific study found that listening to motivating information via podcasts can really strengthen people's resolve. The study found that overweight or obese people who listened to podcasts which gave them information about good nutrition, on how important it is to reach a healthy weight and so on, actually helped people lose half a pound each week over the 12-week study. It makes sense, really. Listening to positive messages that reinforce your ambitions and goals can be really motivating. You may want to try downloading a podcast relevant to your own goal, or investing in a positive-thinking CD to get similar benefits.

Hear the Sounds of Success

Music can be incredibly motivating. When I'm at the gym I can get really energised just by listening to the right music. When you need a boost, try listening to the kind of music that really moves you, anything that stirs you and sparks you up inside! Put it on before you sit down to start work; you'll be surprised how it can give you a buzz. Tina Turner's 'Simply the Best' is one of my personal favourites for this of course! And

Alicia Keys' 'If I ain't got you' was my Olympic song – the words really captured how I felt about my medals.

Reward Yourself

We're going to look at the importance of rewards more in the next chapter. But one really effective way to make sure you stay motivated through each stage of your goal is to give yourself regular incentives. This could be a treat, or a daily reward, or a series of brownie points which, when you've accumulated enough, earn you a bigger reward! If I won a race I'd celebrate with a bar of chocolate or some wine gums, or a Chinese meal. And boy, did I enjoy those treats. Make yourself a list of personal treats and have one after a job well done … And you could always do a list of 'penalties' you have to pay if you don't manage to tick anything off your to-do list.

WHAT TO DO TODAY FOR SUCCESS TOMORROW

✓ *Boost flagging motivation by writing down a list of your reasons for setting yourself the goal in the first place.* How is it going to enhance your life and make you happy? Give yourself 10 good reasons for keeping on your path …

✓ *List all your reasons for losing your motivation* – it's too hard, or you've lost your willpower, or you find it hard to do it by yourself. Sit down and work out some really sensible but effective solutions to these problems.

✓ *Start thinking about the language you use.* For every negative thought or word, offer yourself a positive one in its place.

✓ *Take time out:* a few days off won't stop your progress.

✓ *Devise a list of treats you can give yourself as a reward for sticking to your plan.* Something to put a smile back on your face …

CHAPTER 6

Enjoy the Journey: The Rewards of Perseverance

'Rewards can come in all sorts of different ways. The key is to enjoy the journey you are on – to see each step you take as a reward in itself...'

– Kelly

How do Olympic champions celebrate their victories? I can't answer for anyone else, although just looking at your medals is a thrill. But wow, it blew me away when I came back to the UK after Athens. I never once thought beyond winning a gold medal, but when I landed in the UK, the champagne really started to flow. For someone who doesn't drink a lot at any time, and hadn't at that point had a drink for months – just one on my birthday that year – having one glass of Champagne was enough to last the whole night.

In fact, it was a whirlwind of celebrations on my return from Athens. My mum had arranged a lovely do for friends and family at a local venue. People in my hometown had seen me running for years, so it felt like *their* victory, too. And I also had an amazing homecoming parade. The official number that turned out to greet me was 40,000, but the police report said it was nearer 80,000! We drove through the streets on a fantastic double-decker, and

I'd invited lots of people to join me on the bus – my brothers, sisters, mum, dad, my coach Dave, my friends Kerrie and Tess – in fact, all the people who had played an important part in my life – even my PE teacher from school, Debbie Page. Everyone who had helped me realise my dream was there.

I was overwhelmed with pride and elation as we drove down the road from the Scout Hut in the village to the town of Tonbridge surrounded by thousands of smiling faces, many of them familiar from my childhood and years growing up in Hildenborough – all shouting, waving flags and banners and cheering. It was all brilliant. Celebrating my success with so many people was fantastic. I will never forget it ...

CELEBRATE

Celebrating is important. Marking achievements in your life is important. When you achieve something that has required effort, sacrifice, commitment, it *should* be applauded, it's *worth* celebrating. Of course you feel great inside for having achieved it, but the celebration is the icing on the cake.

Following up any longed-for goal is hard. Everyone experiences those really tough times and occasions when they want to give it all up. Some days you love it, some days you hate it. But if you keep going, you can only reap benefits. That's why marking each victory – each stepping stone successfully manoeuvred – *is* a great cause for celebration. Little treats and prizes you award yourself provide all-important moments of pleasure and acknowledgement which can help keep you going, but also enable you to sit back, take stock and *enjoy the journey.*

'Never postpone enjoyment and happiness until you get to the final destination ...'

– Kelly

Secondly, I think pursuing a goal – however big or small – and achieving it gives you so many wonderful feelings about yourself that they're *rewards* in themselves.

In this chapter I want to look at some of those added extras. When you work steadfastly for something, it has far-reaching effects on you as a person. I suppose it's what they call 'character building'. The whole journey in pursuit of your goal can leave you feeling braver, stronger, more resilient, and doubly confident. And all that has a knock-on effect on the rest of your life. It really does. (I'm living proof.)

WHY NOT REWARD YOURSELF

The Rewards of Rewards

There are good reasons to reward yourself along your journey. According to scientists at ARISE (Associates for Research into the Science of Enjoyment), the experience of pleasure can reduce stress hormones and improve your immune system, helping you fight infections and disease.

The best advice I can give you is to remember that sometimes in life you are allowed to let your hair down or switch off and relax. So often, trying to achieve something can become stressful and make you anxious. Being tearful is common when you are trying to change who you are or what you want to do. I tell you, knowing the amount of tears I cried would definitely change some people's perceptions of me – this seemingly strong woman.

But I think tears and upset are a normal reaction – it shows that something means enough to have a really big effect on you. How you get out of it, though, is the key.

On any journey there will be hard times to face – when things don't go to plan. So do feel proud of yourself if there is something you *have* achieved. So, for even a small achievement, reward yourself with something you enjoy or really want. In fact, why not take your diary or a piece of paper and give yourself half an hour to compile a list of treats or rewards you could give yourself. (Build on that original 'incentives' list we talked about in the last chapter.)

I'm sure there are plenty of things that you would love to do. You can include anything – meals out, spa days, concerts, movies, an afternoon with your favourite glossy magazine, a bottle of wine. Basically you can write down anything you like – but you may want to be disciplined about when you give yourself that reward. For example, when I was in competition, I cut down on my sweets and chocolate intake. If I was racing at a weekend, I would promise myself a big bar of chocolate or a bag of wine gums as a treat.

Make it something you will only have if you *really* feel you have achieved one of your targets or your goal. Remember, even if your goal is to lose weight, food treats are allowed (as long as they're 'treats', not an everyday blowout!).

Lots of my rewards tend to be food-focused. In fact, a good Chinese meal and a bar of chocolate have often been used to mark big achievements in my life!

I remember passing my driving test at the age of 17. I was so excited, and my mum and dad were standing at the front door when I came home, really proud of me. I ripped the L plates off my white Ford Escort and said that I was going to go out and collect the Chinese takeaway Mum and Dad had ordered so we could celebrate. I can't tell you how pleased I was with myself. It was the first time I'd driven on my own. Unfortunately, all didn't quite go to plan. I managed to drive to town and pick up the takeaway, but when I set off back home the car wouldn't start, so I was stranded. I was gutted and it was a bit of an anti-climax when my dad had to come back and pick me up! But we ate the Chinese takeaway eventually, so we still had that celebration ...

I'm not sure athletes use this system of rewards often enough! They don't really celebrate smaller successes. But that's because in sport, the *achievements* themselves are the rewards. It's slightly different to, say, pursuing a work-related goal, when the end point is the promotion or achieving that pay rise – the kind of accomplishments people do celebrate.

When I was in the Army it was a great thrill to be promoted from Private to Lance Corporal, to Corporal, to Sergeant. And because you tend to share rooms in the Army, when you finally get your own bunk (bedroom), you know you've really made it!

But in sport, you're aiming for your own personal best time, or to win a race. It's tough in many ways because there isn't a second-best when you're an athlete. If you've set your sights on winning, nothing else will do. If you've set yourself a goal of running really well tactically, then coming second might be a good reward, but you don't go celebrating that, exactly. But you do always strive to improve on your performance, either in a race or in training, and to reach your own personal targets. You always acknowledge those, because they keep you going.

That's why I'd really recommend recognising each small target you reach – with regular treats and celebrations. They're motivating, they're fun and they give you a big pat on the back for your efforts.

So have a think about what you plan to give yourself. For example, when you lose a certain amount of weight (this doesn't have to mean that you've reached your goal weight), you'll treat yourself to a new pair of jeans. When you, say, hand in an essay, or successfully sit an exam, or finish compiling an impressive new CV, or finish that presentation in time, or manage to bag yourself three interviews for that new type of job you're after, then treat yourself to something nice.

When you're an athlete, tough training is quite like being in a tunnel. You need to be strict with yourself and you can't afford to get distracted by anything else. At the end of anyone's tunnel, the glaring light is a wonderful thing. Make your rewards regular enough to work as an incentive, but don't have so many of them that there's nothing worth working hard for!

Goal-getters Live Longer

Having a purpose in life can help you live longer, according to research published in the journal *Psychosomatic Medicine*. The study found that the people who had goals in life were 57 per cent less likely to die during the study period (five years) than those who didn't have the same kind of direction or purpose. So keep at it. It could add years to your life!

ADDED-EXTRA REWARDS

People ask me if I miss competing. The answer is no, I don't. It was hard – really hard. I don't miss the pain of driving myself to be the very best I could be physically. It was extremely demanding on my body and mind. I know I can never be a better athlete than I was back then. But because I gave it my all, I'm content with that.

When I look over the tough times, both during my athletics career and my years in the Army, I often think, 'I cannot believe I went through all that. How on earth did I do it?' When anyone looks back at their toughest life challenges, they often wonder quite how they survived! But you also think to yourself, 'If I can get through that, I can get through anything!' And that's why pursuing a big goal in life is so empowering. If you're reading this thinking, 'I'm only at the beginning of my journey,' don't worry. You may just need to look back at past achievements and remind yourself of the positive things you *have* done.

I would say there are five key benefits to having stuck to my two big aims of getting into the Army and being an Olympic champion. (And these apply to everyone who has ever set themselves a challenge and pursued it.)

1 IT MAKES YOU TOUGHER

Lining up at the start of race alongside a field of focused, world-class athletes can be really scary. But for me, it's not half as scary as swimming! When you train to be a physical training instructor in the Army, the assumption is that you are good at everything. Swimming and life saving are obligatory. In the Army I had no option but to face my fears, because the truth was I couldn't swim well at all. In fact, I have a real fear of drowning! So, at times, I thought the activities we had to do would get the better of me (and actually kill me).

I remember being completely terrified during a swimming exercise as part of my training course at Aldershot. I had never been a good swimmer, or confident in the water (in fact I could barely swim when I was at school), and here I was, fully dressed in the deep end, having to make a float out of my lightweights (military trousers). This involved treading water while you took off your lightweights, tied knots in the ends of the legs, then, while holding the waist, threw them inside-out so they made a V-shaped float. It was incredibly hard to keep it filled with air, and to stay afloat like that for long.

Time and time again I felt myself going under, swallowing water, gasping for breath, certain I would drown! In sheer desperation I ended up abandoning the exercise and hauling myself out of the pool. The instructor screeched at me to get back in, and threw the lightweights back in while he waited until I went in again. When I did, the same thing happened again – to the point where I knew I would drown if I carried on. So I dragged myself out again and just refused to go on. And there was nothing the instructor could do to make me! God, I was in big trouble, but my life was worth more than that!

Another, even more terrifying exercise, also made me fear for my life. A few years later I had been transferred to the Army Youth Team in Mill Hill in north London. We had to be instructed in various survival skills and adventure training sports in order to be able to take responsibility for the kids' welfare when they were on our camps. Building on other skills involved canoeing on white-water in Nottingham's International Water Sports Centre.

The very idea filled me with horror. Doing it was even worse!

I had to paddle my canoe down the most terrifying rapids, with water churning furiously. As my canoe hit the first obstacle (known as a stopper), I capsized, and the water sucked me under immediately. We had been briefed to keep hold of the canoe if we went in, but I thought, 'Sod that' and I let go of my canoe. The force of the water hurled me down the course like a rag doll. I hit one stopper after another, narrowly avoiding breaking my leg, and swallowing so much water I really thought I would die. When you're sucked under rushing water time and time again, you feel sure that death is inevitable. It was a thousand times worse than I ever thought it was going to be – without doubt the most terrifying experience of my life.

Even though I shudder when I think back, I definitely feel a braver person for these challenges. I wouldn't necessarily choose to go on a kayaking holiday these days, or leap out of a plane into the sea (why do people do that?!?). But knowing I faced my fears and conquered them gives me a huge sense of courage and achievement, both where water is concerned, and also for other potentially uncomfortable or scary situations.

So goals can be great because they can take you out of your comfort zone, make you push yourself that bit further and really find out what you're made of.

My most terrifying moment: Here's a useful test. Think about your most terrifying experiences – those that really took you out of your comfort zone. It might have been standing up in front of people to give a speech or presentation, doing a daredevil bungee jump or similar, giving birth – whatever really put you face-to-face with your fears. Then think about how it empowered you. How proud you were to have done it. (Even if you felt you made a right hash of it, chances are you crossed some massive boundaries even by stepping up to the challenge.) Now's the time to acknowledge to yourself just how character-building that situation really was. How much braver or more capable do you think you are now?

BLAST YOUR RESISTANCE

There are lots of exercises to help you edge out of your comfort zone:

Stand under the shower and, while you're under the water, quickly turn the tap from hot to cold for one second. Do it for a bit longer each day, until you're able to stand under a cold shower for one whole minute. Strange as it may seem, withstanding that cold water blast is actually helping you to extend your comfort zone, and increase your self-control. It's a really useful way to remind yourself that you have the willpower to resist unhelpful temptations, or to keep going when the going gets tough.

2 IT CAN BOOST YOUR WILLPOWER

We talked in the last chapter about how to improve your motivation. It's an area many people struggle with. I'd say my motivation and willpower are both pretty good. They should be. I've spent so many years verbalising and visualising my goals over and over again that I've become pretty adept at firing myself up. I establish what I want, I think about why I want it, and I work out how to go about getting it. *Believing* you can do it is key, though, it keeps you focused on the task ahead.

Think of your willpower as a muscle that gets stronger the more regularly you use it. The more you exercise it, the better it develops and the stronger it gets. Like training, you have to build up gradually but be consistent.

From tomorrow, promise yourself that you will achieve just one task. Make it something really simple that you know you can't fail to do. This could be tidying a drawer, finishing a piece of work, getting up half an hour earlier, cleaning the house before you go to work, paying just one bill, doing some exercise. Once you get into the swing of keeping those promises to yourself, gradually increase your list. In time you'll find the big stuff easier to manage.

(Some experts suggest you put some money in a jar each time you keep a promise to yourself. At the very least, if you stick to it, you'll see the cash increase!)

Can You Resist the Marshmallow?

This scientific study on 'delayed gratification', often called 'the marshmallow test', was first conducted by Stanford University psychology professor Walter Mischel 40 years ago to assess the strength of young children's willpower, and also to see if there was any correlation between that and success in later life.

The test measured how long children, at the age of 4, could delay gratification – by finding out how long they could postpone eating a marshmallow. They were left in a room with the marshmallows and were told they could eat not one but two of them *if* they managed to resist the sweets until the adult returned 20 minutes later.

The results showed that those who resisted for longer had greater confidence, concentration and reliability – and later proved to be more successful in adult life.

When I was 15 I worked in a sweet shop. I love sweets and have a very sweet tooth. On one occasion a woman called Carol, who worked in the shop, had a bet with me about who could last the longest without eating a single sweet. I am so competitive – I was so determined to beat her that I stopped eating sweets for a whole year! It was torture, but I knew from then that I had the willpower to do pretty much anything I set my sights on.

Flex your self-control by seeing if you can resist that cake/bun/TV programme, or any other distracting or unhealthy behaviour, for 20 minutes. Try it over and over again and you will probably see that you have more self-control than you thought!

3   IT GIVES YOU SELF-BELIEF AND CONFIDENCE IN YOUR ABILITIES

I'm not a financial whizz, nor am I naturally good at spelling. And I'll probably never be the world's best cook. But even though I know I may not excel at everything, I know what I am good at (running, for one). Being a good, loyal friend, working with young people, party planning, committing to a task, being creative are a few. And what's more, I know I would have a good stab at most things. I'm confident that if I want something, I can work hard enough to get it. That's because I look at past proof. It's all there in my history. And it's all there in everyone's history. If you look hard enough, you can see what you're good at and where your talents lie, what you've achieved and how you've achieved it. You may need time really to mull this one over – particularly if you can't believe you have achieved anything of note. You have done. And if you need reassurance, ask around: use this quick exercise. Embarrassing as it may seem, stick with it – it's a really useful and confidence-building task. Ask four or five people you know to answer these questions:

1. What's the first thing you think of when you think of me?

2. What is the most interesting thing about me?

3. What do you think I do really well?

4. What would you say are my greatest strengths?

5. What do you think you can learn from me?

It's a really good confidence-booster, and you may find you become aware of talents you didn't know you possessed!

4 IT'S GOOD FOR THOSE AROUND YOU

I've certainly put my friends, family and athletics 'team' through some challenges over the years. All those highs and lows, winning (and losing) races. My friends and family have always stuck by me because they know just how important certain dreams have been to me. They also realise that if I let my dreams drift away or didn't give it 100 per cent, I would be a miserable and unpleasant person to be around! So I strongly believe that when you strive for something everyone close to you goes through it with you. And when you achieve it, other people around you will be happy because *you'll* be a happier person.

We don't always realise the impact we have on other people when we're brought down by our disappointments or frustrations. For example, if you're unhappy about your size, shape, weight, job, then the aura around you, the vibes you give off to other people, can be incredibly negative. In turn, that can be quite draining for them. If the people around you know what you are trying to achieve, they are more likely to understand what you're going through – and may even be able to help you. Those closest to you, who really care for you will – without doubt – want to support you. They can be *part* of it. And at the end of it, you can celebrate together!

5   IT GIVES YOU A SENSE OF FREEDOM

I'm happiest when I'm achieving. Most of us are, really, aren't we? Although we all have different ideas of what it is to achieve.

In athletics, the happiest I have ever been in my life was crossing the finish line of the 1,500 metres at Athens. It was a real dream come true. But it was also a weight off my shoulders! It was a release from the years of hard work and constant drive and focus that had kept me striving hard from the age of 14. It was all behind me.

So, in that respect, fulfilling my goal has given me freedom!

And it's given me other types of freedom as well: it has given me new opportunities, by opening doors for me that would never otherwise have been open. My Olympic triumphs have enabled me to meet interesting, influential people, to pursue other dreams. And I feel that achieving those medals at the relatively mature age of 34 was an advantage in certain respects: I had the life experience and wisdom that the 20-year-old me hadn't had, and which I could build on. So trust me, it's never too late!

To a certain extent, people put you on their own kind of pedestal when you do something at such a high level in such a public way – such as winning two

Olympic gold medals. In sport, nothing can ever get any better or bigger than that. It gives you that sense of 'Wow, look at what I've done!' People want to hear from you, they believe in you, they trust in you. So it gives you a lift, opens up new horizons – and also brings new responsibilities.

That's what happened to me.

Whoever you are, and whatever you are trying to achieve, always remember that reaching the end of the journey may give you a whole new lease on life too.

When you re-train and suddenly find all sorts of new career paths open to you, the world becomes your oyster.

And when you get out of debt, or decide to cash in your savings and see the world or start a new life abroad, there's a huge sense of liberty.

Above all, reaching a goal gives you a new kind of independence because it means that, along the way, you have grown in knowledge, expertise and experience. You're braver, more confident, and have greater determination than you had before.

And with all that behind you, you really can fly ...

LIFE'S A CELEBRATION: ENJOYING THE JOURNEY

I'm probably not the best person to be talking about fine-tuning your work/life balance, because I'm not sure how balanced mine is! (Or perhaps that makes me the ideal person to offer advice?)

The truth is, my head doesn't often take a break, and these days my work – what with my charities, my mentoring roles, sponsorship commitments and so on – is fairly non-stop. Plus, alongside all that, I'm on a business course and am working on my new business ideas – developing my own brand of goods. So I'm on the go all the time.

As an elite athlete, I rarely went on holiday because I was training or racing virtually the whole time. That's why holidays are one of the things I most enjoy since retiring from athletics (when I get time). It's fantastic not having to worry about what I'm eating or drinking or what time I'm going to bed while I'm away. But I do have to *force* myself to switch off (both my head and my phone) when I get there!

You could say I'm a workaholic – and that is really *not* healthy. However, I do know when I have blown a gasket – and at that stage I love nothing more than to lie on the sofa with a Chinese, watching trashy TV. In truth, I love what I do, but I admit that it sometimes gets overwhelming just trying to fit everything in.

We all get into that cycle of doing, doing, doing. Once you add in those additional pressures many people have, such as looking after kids, or travelling abroad with work, even commuting every day, then you can see why life can be overwhelmingly frantic. At best, monotonous. How many times have you kept on going, feeling like you're on a treadmill, wondering to yourself *when am I going to have any enjoyment in my life?*

If this sounds familiar, then please look at your work/life balance. This is one area where I do not recommend you follow my lead! I'm writing this in the hope that *I* will take a leaf out of my *own* book! Spend time working out how to reshuffle your commitments around, or offload certain burdens, and take that long-overdue holiday. At the very least, resolve right here, right now to give yourself 30 minutes 'me-time' every day. (This is all possible – look back at Chapter 2 for some tips.)

In the meantime, it's really important to look at how much happiness and pleasure you are deriving from your life every day – *just as it is*. Today. Right now. Because if you put off feeling happy and good about yourself, then you're missing out on right now. Plus you may find it difficult to feel really good when you've got there.

What I'm talking about – and what psychologists tell us is crucial for overall happiness – is learning to enjoy *living in the moment*. That doesn't mean putting up with what you have right now and not bothering to strive for something new and fresh and exciting. Rather, it means that by learning to savour the good elements of the journey you are also living for today.

Put it like this: if your goal is to lose body fat and shape up, and you regard that whole journey as miserable, a time of deprivation and self-denial (which you can't wait to be over), then it's pretty much doomed. Instead, aim to see the good and enjoyable aspects of what you're doing. You're not denying yourself junk food and cakes; you're treating yourself to top-quality food – like fresh fruits, bursting with vitamins. You're savouring new, delicious flavours and textures. You're filling your body with the best fuel out there! Your waistband is looser, you have more energy to play with the kids, or run for the bus now, and you can feel your body getting stronger and leaner every day. You're looking better. Surely that has to be worth it!

And if you're trying to get a new job, aim to regard each step as a positive one, taking you closer to your overall goal. So, even if you've just been through a really tough interview and didn't get the job, try to extract the good bits from the experience. You've learned from it; it's been good practice; you'll be wiser/better prepared next time.

I'd Like to Thank ...

Psychology experts recommend keeping a *gratitude list* – it's designed to help you enjoy life right now, rather than take it for granted. So each night before you go to bed, make a mental note of five things for which you're grateful, or which make you happy. (Make it 10 if you're feeling particularly good!) You can focus this gratitude list on your goal itself, or on life in general. It could be a delicious low-fat meal you really enjoyed, or a brisk walk in the park, a great workout class, the fantastic feeling of accomplishment when you finished that essay or presentation, or drinking a cool glass of wine when the sun is setting.

From right now, make it a rule to take a few minutes every day to stop and actually enjoy 'the moment' – and savour your life. These could be the moments when you're totally absorbed in something – cooking or listening to music or reading a really great book, or when you're looking out of the window at the trees while you're doing your daily commute.

While you're working hard on creating that great future, don't forget to enjoy the present – the life you have today ...

WHAT TO DO TODAY FOR SUCCESS TOMORROW

✓ *Reward yourself for each step you successfully complete that is taking you nearer to your goal.* Write a list of rewards/celebrations so they're there in black and white.

✓ *Motivate yourself further by acknowledging the character-building element of pursuing your goal.* What are you gaining in terms of personal strengths?

✓ *Boost your willpower and courage further by regularly taking yourself out of your comfort zone.*

✓ *Enjoy the journey* – keep a gratitude diary listing all the best moments of each day.

Conclusion

'*Sometimes in your life you have to make sacrifices. There is no easy road to success or achievement, but with a bit of dedication and realistic targets you can make them happen ...*'

– from my book
Black, White and Gold

Right at this moment I am working on my very latest project.

I have a bulging file containing cuttings from newspapers and journals, useful numbers, facts and figures, inspiring articles and pictures of samples that I've come across which have helped nudge forward my idea. I've refined the various ideas and have decided where I'm going next: I intend to launch my own lifestyle brand, one that's based on my name – which will, very broadly, involve different products, services, events, companies and so on, all within the areas of health, well-being, fitness, leisure and sport.

That's the big picture, anyway. The plans are firming up. They most definitely will be tweaked again here and there as I work on them further, but the vision is there, and it's really taking shape. I've given myself a five-year goal – by which time I hope to be in business!

Having a new venture to work on has really fired me up again (now that my charity work and mentoring projects are well established). Business is really unfamiliar territory for me, and it's been the most massive learning curve. I'm not sure how long it will take before my projects start coming to fruition (it would be great to be up and running by the time you're reading this book), but I'm keeping my feet firmly in reality, working hard and learning more day by day. I have been on a business course at the Institute of Directors. (If I'm honest, at first I sat there thinking, 'I haven't got a clue what you're saying!') But I've learnt a lot, and now I can see my new career starting to take shape. I have met people who have given me great advice along the way. (One day I will be able to thank them properly.) And I have brought a new team on board in the licensing and TV industry. Who knows where it will all go, but if you don't start somewhere, you don't get anywhere!

Like many people out there who are working on ideas outside their 'day job', this is a project I've had to pursue alongside other commitments (which in my case occupy me 7 a.m.–1 a.m.!). But I've been taking it one stage at a time – and have heeded my own 'step by step' advice that you've been reading about in this book!

The ultimate goal? Well, let's just say it would be great if my CV read 'Dame Kelly Holmes – Soldier, Athlete, Double Olympic Champion, Businesswoman ...'

ON YOUR MARKS

Now that you've reached the end of this book, I hope you may have found something to help you feel inspired to move forward on some of your own ideas and plans. I hope it has helped you question your hopes and expectations, and ideally to find a few solutions to problems such as where (on earth) to start. I wanted the book to provide a kind of 'template for change,' a step-by-step programme to get you closer to the life you want to live, doing what you really want to do.

So my advice is: keep thinking, but make sure you start *doing* as well. Don't let fear of failure, or lack of energy, or sheer laziness hold you back. You've read this far in the book, so you must be looking for change. The only way to move forward is to *just go for it*. Now!

GET SET

You don't have to spend all day 'getting started' – it's a mistake to put things off because you don't think you'll have long enough to achieve anything. Don't sit around waiting for the 'ideal' moment to arrive: make it happen.

The fact is, most of us want more from life. We want to feel valued. And we need to feel that life is worth living! At the end of the day, each of us has very different opportunities, but we all have the right to a better life – the right to dream, the right to hope.

Whether we choose to make that change is down to us, though. But pushing through those boundaries and fighting for our achievements really will make all the difference.

I know I have been successful in my life. I know I have had a talent in sport that took me to the highest level. But I have also cried, been in pain, felt sick with worry at the thought of letting people down. I have felt vulnerable and struggled to cope at times, so unsure of what the future held.

Those feelings affect us all at some stage. But I do believe there is always light at the end of the tunnel. And unless you try, you will never find it!

GO!

I really hope you feel as excited about your future as I do about mine. I hope that having read this book you feel more confident about your ideas, and about changing direction in your life. Above all, please don't ever be afraid to give things a go. At the very least, you can say you tried. And that's an achievement in itself.

Believe in yourself.

Love, Kelly x

twitter@damekellyholmes.co.uk
www.kellyholmes.co.uk

Notes

Notes

Notes

Notes

Notes

Notes

Notes

Notes

Notes

Notes

Hay House Titles of Related Interest

Core Balance Diet,
by Marcelle Pick

Life Lessons,
by Lesley Garner

One-Minute Mindfulness,
by Simon Parke

Success Intelligence,
by Robert Holden

Supercoach,
by Michael Neill

JOIN THE HAY HOUSE FAMILY

As the leading self-help, mind, body and spirit publisher in the UK, we'd like to welcome you to our family so that you can enjoy all the benefits our website has to offer.

 EXTRACTS from a selection of your favourite author titles

 LISTEN to a range of radio interviews and our latest audio publications

 **LATEST NEWS** Keep up with the latest news from and about our authors

iPHONE APPS Download your favourite app for your iPhone

 **COMPETITIONS, PRIZES & SPECIAL OFFERS** Win extracts, money off, downloads and so much more

 **CELEBRATE YOUR BIRTHDAY** An inspiring gift will be sent your way

 ATTEND OUR AUTHOR EVENTS Be the first to hear about our author events

 **HAY HOUSE INFORMATION** Ask us anything, all enquiries answered

join us online at **www.hayhouse.co.uk**

292B Kensal Road, London W10 5BE
T: 020 8962 1230 E: info@hayhouse.co.uk

We hope you enjoyed this Hay House book.
If you would like to receive a free catalogue featuring additional
Hay House books and products, or if you would like information
about the Hay Foundation, please contact:

Hay House UK Ltd
292B Kensal Road • London W10 5BE
Tel: (44) 20 8962 1230; Fax: (44) 20 8962 1239
www.hayhouse.co.uk

***

Published and distributed in the United States of America by:
Hay House, Inc. • PO Box 5100 • Carlsbad, CA 92018-5100
Tel: (1) 760 431 7695 or (1) 800 654 5126;
Fax: (1) 760 431 6948 or (1) 800 650 5115
www.hayhouse.com

***

Published and distributed in Australia by:
Hay House Australia Ltd • 18/36 Ralph Street • Alexandria, NSW 2015
Tel: (61) 2 9669 4299, Fax: (61) 2 9669 4144
www.hayhouse.com.au

***

Published and distributed in the Republic of South Africa by:
Hay House SA (Pty) Ltd • PO Box 990 • Witkoppen 2068
Tel/Fax: (27) 11 467 8904
www.hayhouse.co.za

***

Published and distributed in India by:
Hay House Publishers India • Muskaan Complex • Plot No.3
B-2 • Vasant Kunj • New Delhi - 110 070
Tel: (91) 11 41761620; Fax: (91) 11 41761630
www.hayhouse.co.in

***

Distributed in Canada by:
Raincoast • 9050 Shaughnessy St • Vancouver, BC V6P 6E5
Tel: (1) 604 323 7100
Fax: (1) 604 323 2600

***

Sign up via the Hay House UK website to receive the Hay House
online newsletter and stay informed about what's going on with your
favourite authors. You'll receive bimonthly announcements
about discounts and offers, special events, product highlights,
free excerpts, giveaways, and more!
www.hayhouse.co.uk